The Call is both a delight and engag
mission and discipleship in their local
teaching with a context of a postmode
thinking, church growth, discipleship, deep worship and evangelism. This writing is a jewel that is helpful to any pastoral leader, even as it unfolds the story of a local church in Lower Burrell PA.

- The Very Rev. Henry L. Thompson
Dean and President of Trinity School for Ministry, Ambridge PA

In *The Call*, Cletus Hull tells the story of a church in its context. His description of Trinity Church's ministry of evangelism and discipleship offers insight to other churches as they seek God's direction for ministry in our contexts. Dr. Hull demonstrates how evangelism and discipleship interrelate. He shows that they are founded on Scripture and classic Christian teaching while being empowered by the Holy Spirit. This book is an invitation to engage in a theology of healthy church growth in the world where we live. As Pastor Hull shows how Trinity implements this theology, he encourages us to put it into practice where we are.

- Rev. Dr. John Breon
Pastor, First United Methodist Church, Durant, OK

Cletus Hull has given a perceptive analysis of church growth principles applied to a post-modern setting. His description of the application to Trinity United Christian Church in Lower Burrell PA is encouraging and challenging for those readers seeking transformation in their own congregations.

- Rev. Dr. David Mansfield
Pastor of Benton Christian Church, Benton, PA

This book by my good friend Dr. Cletus Hull is an excellent read that is scholarly, yet clear and practical. As C.H. Spurgeon once said, "Leave some cookies on the bottom shelf", implying that that you should always make your message, which this book does, challenging yet easy to understand.

- Rev. Rex Petty
Pastor, Faith Tabernacle, Liberal, KS

Dr. Hull is both a practitioner and a theologian. In *The Call*, he provides a plan for his church to move forward in evangelism and discipleship based on theological and contextual reflection. The reader is invited to join the thought process behind this church's strategic plan.

- Dr. Gary C. Bailey
President of Biblical Life Institute, Freeport, PA

A moving historical overview of the region. The timeline of Trinity United Christian Church includes future ideas for growth. It was a very intriguing look into the church.

- Richard Callender
Mayor of Lower Burrell, PA

God certainly seems to gift men and women with spiritual gifts that keep the church moving forward. Cletus is uniquely gifted as a local parish pastor and as a theologian. How fortunate is the church to have this theologian in residence. This thoughtful survey of the ministry is no less than the story of God at work in humanity and the world. The Reverend Hull offers us this prophetic piece that identifies where God has been, where God is, and points us to where God will be. I am grateful for this servant of the Servant Church and for the saints that have formed this flock over the ages. This faithful work blesses the church at home and models a way for others to follow.

- Rev. Thaddaeus Allen
Regional Minister of the Christian Church (Disciples of Christ) in West Virginia and Pennsylvania

I truly enjoyed this book and how it relates the times of Jesus to this postmodern era. The history of Trinity United Christian Church and the area where it is located was fascinating to me. This book is a great resource for the methodology for church growth through discipleship and evangelism. There are step by step examples shared by the author's own experiences in leading his church through the process of spiritual growth, and the importance of laity in that growth. There are great tips for evangelizing to the postmodern generation through multiple venues that include music, prayer, small groups, silence and drama. It's exciting to follow TUCC through their growth and their efforts to be a model to other churches in how to reach this generation and those to come. A really interesting and engaging read!

- Karen Snair
Executive Director at Allegheny Valley Association of Churches, Natrona Heights, PA

The Call came to me at just the right time, beginning a new pastorate at a lovely, deeply "Traditional" congregation. Cletus paints a clear picture of the Church's struggle to reach all generations in this "Postmodern" culture. His road map for evangelism and discipleship will shape this pastor's call to build God's church.

- Rev. John H. Owen
Pastor, First Christian Church, Greensburg, PA

Pastor Cletus makes an honest and brave attempt to lay out a vision for ministry that incorporates pastor and congregation in order that authentic biblical discipleship and evangelism can move forward and thrive in the 21st century.

- Rev. John Bailey
Pastor, Christ Our Hope Anglican Church, Natrona Heights, PA

Pastor Hull has captured the essence of what is truly needed in the church today; a commitment to evangelism and discipleship, in a post-modern era. I pray that all who read this book will capture this vision.

- Dean Gartland
CEO and President of Washington City mission, Washington PA

THE CALL

MY MISSION AND OUR MINISTRY AT TRINITY UNITED CHRISTIAN CHURCH, LOWER BURRELL PA

CLETUS L. HULL, III

WORD ASSOCIATION PUBLISHERS
www.wordassociation.com
1.800.827.7903

Printed in the United States of America.

ISBN: 978-1-63385-307-2

Library of Congress Control Number: 2019903460

Designed and published by
Word Association Publishers
205 Fifth Avenue
Tarentum, Pennsylvania 15084

www.wordassociation.com
1.800.827.7903

TABLE OF CONTENTS

FOREWORD

Pastoral ministry is not for the faint of heart. I once asked an elderly pastor with over 50 years of pastoral experience in numerous churches what the secret to his longevity was. He replied in slow and punctuated words, "Thick skin!" The pastoral image of the servant of God as a shepherd tending to passive sheep is misleading. Those sheep as Jesus said are sometimes wolves wearing disguises. The Apostle Paul does not candy coat ministry when he say in Ephesians, "Finally be strong in the Lord and in his mighty power. Put on the full armor of God so that you can stand against the devil's schemes." (Eph. 6:10)

I first met Cletus in seminary as a young man trying to find his way in the work of the church. I recall numerous conversations we had after he became a student pastor in a well- established traditional church. Cletus was surprised to find hostilities there. He encountered ambushes by those in power and not a few landmines when changing sacred traditions. As I read his book **The Call** I could not help but think of how formative his student pastorate was in preparing him for the ministry he has had at Trinity United Christian Church. Leading traditional churches through change is not for the weak of heart either.

Cletus has always had this ability to be a non- anxious presence that has kept him and the church on track while giving grace filled guidance.

It is inspiring to read how Reverend Hull has helped two very traditional yet different churches to merge into one vital congregation. He has been able to motivate people who were entrenched in their own cultures and communities to higher levels of growth while keeping the ancient story of the gospel. I appreciate how Pastor Hull has been uncompromising in his biblical and evangelical foundation yet open to different presentations of the gospel message. I am amazed at how he was able to start a Saturday night youth lead service called the ROCK while at the same time attempting to minister to those who were more comfortable in a traditional service.

At the core of Rev. Dr. Hull's ministry has been the emphasis upon discipleship. The use of small house groups as well as fostering intergenerational ministry has laid the foundation for his churches transformation. His methodologies for reaching the post-modern generation have included drama, music, a coffee house, inductive bible study, mentoring and accountability. The leadership of Trinity United Christian Church expected God to do great things, and was committed to reaching seeking people and gave youth ministry a high priority.

As Reverend Hull stated, "We have learned at Trinity United Christian Church that when a pastor, led by the Holy Spirit, is willing to pay the price for using influence to lead a church to plan a strategy and establish goals, renewal can happen." Cletus Hull is one who has paid the price, stayed the course, prayed and seen God work.

Dr. Hull asked the question of church leaders, "Are we zealous enough, convicted enough, passionate enough, determined enough to do the work of evangelism? Do we love the Lord enough to obey the Great Commission?" Cletus Hull has been that kind of leader for his church. His courage and humility in the work of congregational renewal I admire. I commend this book to you and trust you will find it insightful and challenging as I have.

- Rev. Dr. David Mansfield

ACKNOWLEDGMENTS

THE CALL is a culmination of a lifetime of serving the church in mission for the Lord. God has called me to the local church and I dedicated my life to this endeavor. So, you might say that this book is many years in the making. It certainly would not have been possible without the many God-moments I have experienced since I began my service as a pastor in the Christian ministry. That includes First Christian Church, Marianna PA; First Christian, Washington PA; and the ministry experience I have encountered at Trinity United Christian Church, Lower Burrell PA. I began working at Trinity on January 1, 1996 and I would not trade anything for the experiences and friendships of my years there.

Additionally, I am thinking of my parents, Sunday School teachers, parents of childhood friends, high school teachers, and many others whose faith and commitment to the church made a lasting impression on me at an early age. I am thinking of college and seminary professors whose ability to balance faith and scholarship was a source of encouragement, and theological mentors whose lives were models of what I desired to become. These are the hidden influences that have made the writing of this book possible. To all my pastor friends, in the Christian Church (Disciples of Christ) in the Pennsylvania Region who I met through the years—each one took the time to invest and care about a pastor who give his best efforts in life to the ministry. Thank you!

As the old saying goes, "no man is an island," and I want to thank the people at Trinity Church in Lower Burrell who continued with me through the years to make this book a reality in ministry—people such as Tim Woods, Janet Furer, Rich Schachte, Bob Schultz, and the Trinity church family who persevered in all our times together. You are a special breed and seldom receive "thanks" for your tireless love, grace, and giving to the church. I also want to express love and gratitude for my wife, Bridget. She is my best friend and a gift. I met her at this church and her own ministry experience in the church and music gives me an eye for what is real in life. Thus, the book's dedication to her.

Most of all, I recognize and thank the Lord Jesus Christ, for Whom I minister, and without Whom I would have no life, ministry or eternal hope.

Soli Deo Gloria!

Cletus Hull

These pastors in the Christian Church (Disciples of Christ) are a few of the colleagues with whom I have enjoyed the ministry in all the years.

INTRODUCTION

A clear mandate is given from the Bible to all Christians about evangelism and discipleship. Jesus commanded His disciples before He left this earth, with these words: "Therefore go and make disciples of all nations, baptizing them in the name of the Father and of the Son and of the Holy Spirit, teaching them to obey all I have commanded you" (Matt. 28:19-20).[1] For two thousand years the church has been motivated by these words from Jesus. The mission of the church is to make disciples of all nations. This book is based on the thesis that God wants Trinity United Christian Church (TUCC) to grow and make disciples in our community and the world.

Drive around New Kensington, Pennsylvania, and you will quickly discover a city that is in decline. New Kensington is typical among western Pennsylvania towns, in large part due to its location along the rivers leading into Pittsburgh. The booming steel mills and coal mines that lined this valley were in economic despair. People moved south and west to follow employment opportunities. On the other hand, the town next door, Lower Burrell, reflects a gathering place for families who

1 *New International Version* [of the Holy Bible] (Grand Rapids: Zondervan, 1991). All Scripture is taken from this English translation, unless otherwise specified.

wish to raise children in a residential environment rather than the urban atmosphere that pervades New Kensington.

Trinity United Christian Church (TUCC) evolved out of a 110-year-old congregation that was situated in the center of old New Kensington. This congregation took a bold step of faith. They bought fourteen acres of land in Lower Burrell, in a section of the community earmarked for growth. Within one mile of the new church property there are several new housing developments. As the only Protestant church in the Braeburn Heights area, our responsibility is to reach out to souls for Christ in our own backyard.

TUCC represents the merger of two congregations in 1993. This was a major step for TUCC. Likewise, the church has added (by faith) church staff to facilitate growth. These church leaders have been visionary and courageous. They are willing to take risks. They have sought ways to touch a new generation of people. The church has come a long way toward fulfilling God's commission.

This reflects significant growth over the past twenty-five years. I have served at TUCC since 1996, first as the Associate Pastor, and have been, since 2001, the Senior Pastor. I feel responsible, as their spiritual leader, to move TUCC into the twenty-first century as a church that will make a difference. Thus, the purpose of this book developes a proposal for church growth, both numerically and spiritually. I will address the need to develop a workable plan to build a healthy, growing church.

This focus of ministry for TUCC is divided into three parts. Part One provides us a cultural and economic excursus of Pennsylvania (overall) and the surrounding communities of TUCC. The analysis shows the implications for spiritual and numerical growth at TUCC. It will help us to understand the people we are trying to reach with the Gospel, thus aiding in our strategies in developing methodologies for church growth. In addition to the community makeup surrounding TUCC, it is imperative that we look at the history of this church. TUCC is a merger of two churches, each with its own history. Here, we focus on the implications of that merger, its pastoral leadership before and after the merger, and the implications for church growth in the twenty-first century.

Part Two provides the biblical foundation from which to motivate TUCC to evangelize and disciple, the components necessary for church growth. The biblical foundation for evangelism finds its definitive roots in the New Testament Gospels—in the ministries of both John the Baptist (the forerunner to Jesus) and Jesus. Evangelism after the establishment of the Church is illustrated all throughout the Book of Acts. The biblical foundations for discipleship also discovers its definitive roots in the New Testament Gospels, focusing on the new order of discipleship instituted by Jesus Christ. In the Epistles, Paul continues the concept of discipleship as demonstrated by Jesus. Paul's focus of discipleship stimulates church growth inwardly through the spiritual maturation of every believer. Based upon the biblical foundations for evangelism and discipleship, I propose a theology for church growth. This theology encompasses a theology of evangelism and discipleship in the context of a postmodern, western society.

Part Three sets forth a strategy for spiritual growth at TUCC. This requires the development of a methodology of church growth specifically for TUCC. It is important to first consider the traditional church at TUCC as well as the growing postmodern influence in the church. The target area for church growth is the postmodern sect of our society, which means that evangelism and discipleship methodologies must be developed within a postmodern context. The strategy includes an operational plan that includes a mission statement, core values, and goals to focus the congregation on evangelism and discipleship for continued growth. These components are then presented through practical implementation resulting from the previous programs. Some areas of practical implementation that are discussed include contemporary worship services, small groups ministry, empowering the laity for ministry, and the cultivation and assimilation of new members.

Jesus calls us to go into the world and be His witnesses. We are to share our faith and invite others into His Kingdom. My desire in THE CALL firmly remains to aspire to move and inspire the church members to become intentionally involved in introducing Jesus to others and discipling them to truly follow Him.

PART ONE

BACKGROUND OF TUCC AND ITS SURROUNDING COMMUNITIES

CHAPTER ONE

LOWER BURRELL AND ITS SURROUNDING COMMUNITIES

I feel that Pennsylvania is "stretching" to connect with the postmodern world. It is a state in which life and culture have changed very little in the past thirty years. Many traditionalists adore and prefer this lifestyle. In the Keystone state, the Amish and the Pennsylvania Dutch culture survives from the 1800s. The phrase "Keep it simple" actually means, "Do not complicate our lives." In other words, "Do not change anything."

Although Pennsylvania is part of the technological world, the mindset of the culture is embedded in the past. One must keep in mind that Pennsylvania is a historical state. It was the second state to join the union. Many people settled here first, and there are numerous churches that are more than two hundred years old. Not many places in the United States can claim such a history. Most of the churches in Pennsylvania are small congregations with small town mentalities. Over 80 percent of the churches are considered small (one hundred members or less).

Living in western Pennsylvania, which is known as the "rust belt" (because of the decline of the steel and coal industries), can be a challenge for a pastor. Motivating people to higher levels of church growth, while keeping the ancient story of the Gospel, can be a struggle. Most people are entrenched in their own cultures and communities. Many small towns are centers of parochialism. To understand the congregation there is a need to understand its context and culture. Jesus tells a parable in Matthew 13:1-9, about a sower of seeds and the four different soils on which the seeds fell. The communities that make up and surround New Kensington and Lower Burrell are comprised of various "soils" that impact the way ministry is received. Recognizing the reality of the soil will enable the church to achieve the vision God is unfolding to His people. Understanding the background will be our road-map for change and growth.

The topography of the land may have led to this fractured environment. Pennsylvania is a rural state where most people enjoy living in the natural surroundings of nature, rather than in a modern urban environment. "The mountains 'played an important role in the growth of Pennsylvania's major characteristics: a diversified economy, a heterogeneous society and sectional politics.'"[2] Pennsylvania has more people who are born, live, and die in the same town than any other state. Likewise, it is a state that is proud of tradition. Many pivotal historical events have occurred, such as the Liberty Bell (Philadelphia), the Civil War (Gettysburg), and William Penn's *Holy Experiment.*

2 Philip Klein, A History of Pennsylvania (Pennsylvania State University); quoted in "It All Started in 1681 with Penn," The Tribune Review, n.p. [cited 12 Aug. 2002]. Online: http://www.pittsburglive.com/x /tribune-review/specialreports/regionalism/startwithpenn.html.

THE RELIGIOUS AND CULTURAL HISTORY OF PENNSYLVANIA

In the 1600s, Europe had become a hotbed for religious dissent. Traditionalists fought non-conformists for power. Churches began to persecute each other. The majority groups in religion controlled the political power and punished citizens in their midst. Hence, kings and emperors believed that dissenters would fare better in the new world, where innovation and ideas could be employed.

William Penn, a Quaker, took the challenge. Born, with privilege, into wealth and aristocracy, he received a large area of land as a gift from the king of England. Here, the founder of Pennsylvania and a man ahead of his time, birthed *The Holy Experiment*. *The Holy Experiment* was "to put the kingdom of God into actual operation in the world. The Experiment was an affirmation of the Divine Light in every person, whatever their religion or race, which allowed all people to live in peace."[3] To Penn, people were to care for each other, no matter their background. He took seriously the message of "love your enemies" from Jesus' Sermon on the Mount. He was a pacifist and believed that warfare on any level was wrong. "He believed that with virtuous people and a virtuous government there should be no trouble . . . and that perhaps the colony would be an 'example to the nations.'"[4] Penn believed that with good people and the hand of God, a good government could be established. His noble dream was to create a colony in which freedom of worship was a virtue. Penn used his political influence to campaign for religious freedom and other principles of liberal government. He desired to create a new society based on wider freedoms and

3 Corrine McLaughlin and Gordon Davidson, "The Esoteric Side of the Founding of America," *In Context* 3 (Summer 1983): 7. Cited 12 Aug. 2002. Online: http://www.context.org/ICLIB/IC03/CoriGord.htm.

4 Edwin B. Bronner, *William Penn's "Holy Experiment"* (New York: Temple University Publications, 1962), 12.

a sense of peace. Penn's colony was founded on the fundamental principles of American civil life.

The people who traveled to this colony were very religious and democratic in spirit. In time, Pennsylvania became a haven for minority religious sects from Germany, Holland, Scandinavia, and Great Britain. People worshipped God according to the dictates of their consciences. The churches were congregational and tightly knit organizations. Religious tolerance was accepted from the beginning and incorporated into the founding purpose. There was no reason to suspect that *The Holy Experiment* would fail. The settlers were optimistic about their future. With plenty of fertile land and a mandate guaranteeing freedom of worship, the colony grew rapidly. Many descendants of those folks are still here.

Church life is a large aspect of the Pennsylvania culture and the ethnic families who migrated from Europe. People will not easily give up their traditions. In fact, they will vehemently fight for their beliefs, even if it means having only five to ten people in a congregation. One cultural example is the "shoo-fly" pie of the Pennsylvania Dutch. It is a creation of leftover meals. Nothing is thrown away. Thrift and frugality are virtues. The people are proud of the simplicity of their lives. There is a strong spirit of independence among the inhabitants. This attitude was inherited directly from the original occupants of this colony.

The early founders had a disdain for government and centralized authority, which produced a lack of cooperation among people.[5] With these aspects in mind, although tolerance and diversity were encouraged, a fragmented society developed. This thinking flowed into the churches and created loyal adherents; however, their localism did not cater to the openness of new

5 Ibid., 254.

ideas. Many of the same settlers who fled Europe because of religious persecution, now refused to compromise their own passionately held religious convictions. They enthusiastically supported Penn's effort to create a "city on a hill" for faith, yet, they unconsciously promoted division.

Life is more complex than the idealists believe. The enlightened colonial leaders believed that good people would do the will of God and obey the Scriptures' highest teachings. With so many diverse religious sects in the colony, groups clustered themselves together and created their own fractured societies. Church divisions do not build congregations. Religious persecutions among Christians leave stained memories that harbor resentment and anger for generations to come. *The Holy Experiment* did not accomplish its utopian goals. Its failure was not because of William Penn, but because of the lack of cooperation among churches and religious groups. This experiment failed because of mulish people, not God. Today, Penn's original pragmatism and ecumenical spirit has a hard path to tread in this state.

THE ECONOMIC HISTORY OF PITTSBURGH

At the beginning of the nineteenth century, Pittsburgh, a blue collar city, was built squarely on industry and factory work. The region became a leader in America's industrial production. This work dominated Pittsburgh's economy for over a century. It was an industrial giant producing steel, iron, aluminum, and glass. Smokestacks billowing coal ash covered the atmosphere. The industrial region generated many well paying blue-collar jobs. As a result of its location for river transportation and its coal deposits, Pittsburgh became one of America's most industrialized cities.

However, its preeminent size became its own problem. The world's steel and coal industry was in trouble. Sales plummeted and companies declined. Though led by prudent people, an unyielding corporate structure created a hostile atmosphere. Companies began to merge and close. Industry declined while corporations downsized, relocated, or consolidated. Steel played a smaller role in the world market.

Foreign competition also took the steel companies by surprise. The price of domestic steel far surpassed foreign production and companies turned to other sources. Labor costs and the failure to modernize led to the collapse of the steel industry. Eventually, the three rivers that flow in and out of the "steel city" became lined with closed mines. Through the years, conflicts between labor and management were strained.

The dissolution of the industry caused many people to find themselves unemployed. They were barely making enough to support themselves and their families. Skills, ethnicity, and incomes began to separate people from each other. Isolated mill towns carved out their own distinct personalities. "Few of these mill-town workers ever left their small-town world, and even fewer looked to Pittsburgh for leadership or inspiration."[6] Decades of isolation and conflict have taken its toll. Endless union strikes and layoffs reflected the worsening economy. A feeling of powerlessness has reduced Pittsburgh to meager levels of growth and prosperity. Industry never became a cohesive and united influence in the region. Downtown storefronts were vacant and the streets virtually empty at night. Though the rest of the country was doing well, Pittsburgh was crippled by its own recession.

6 Carl I. Meyerbuber, *Less Than Forever: The Rise and Decline of Union Solidarity in Western Pennsylvania* (Selinsgrove, PA: Susquehanna University Press, 1987), 12.

Older Industrial Pittsburgh

The rise and decline of the industrial revolution is a topic frequently discussed and examined. Pittsburgh was the economic capital of the region but the wealth had not been equally distributed to the surrounding communities. Here is a case scenario that represents the Pittsburgh area:

> New Kensington had been Alcoa's center of production for more than half a century, and *many believed it always would be* [emphasis mine]. After the war, declining production and reductions in the labor force indicated otherwise. Shop closings threatened . . . more jobs. On July 1, 1970, Alcoa announced the termination of its manufactured-products division and the closing of the New Kensington works. By March 31, 1971, the closings had been accomplished.[7]

Every small town has a story like this one. It is the story of this region. Hence, the economic history of Pittsburgh is also the history of its surrounding communities. In the past

7 Ibid., 205.

fifty years, numerous companies redirected their resources. That new direction closed businesses or took them to other places in the United States. With the big economic downturn, manufacturing and steel companies went bankrupt. In addition, industrial work was often hazardous. This was true in both coal mines and steel mills. With other options available for work, younger adults chose less deadly occupations. A malaise slowly took the psyche of the people. Pittsburgh became vulnerable. It hit the pocketbooks and then their hearts. A way of life was dying a slow death. The obituary was being written for western Pennsylvania.

However, not all is doom and gloom. Though the city lost its position as one of the world's largest industrial producers, in the 1980s, a new era—information technology—was born. This emphasis required a complete transformation of its economic system. Today, in the Oakland section of the city, where most of the colleges and universities reside, computer science is a favorite major of many students; consequently, many technology companies are relocating to Pittsburgh. Corporate Pittsburgh is preparing for a post-industrial future. An emphasis is to keep brain drain from occurring. If the area can encourage their best and brightest students to stay, there is hope for a prosperous tomorrow. Entrepreneurship and capital investments are being encouraged. The long-term goal of the city's leadership is that this computer renaissance will birth rejuvenation and new hope to western Pennsylvania.

Increased flexibility and less red tape are placing decisions in the hands of capable local people. Pittsburgh's future is tied to the success of these new developments. The area is weathering the economic storm because it is diversifying. There are stronger numbers in finance, health, and business. The mayors of Pittsburgh and the governors of the state are working to revive the economy and population of the area. Small miracles of growth in western Pennsylvania are emerging. The area is encouraged that these new methods will prove to work for the good of families and communities. As "big steel" produced years of prosperity, now new risk-takers are creating new paths in technology. As businesses emerge from the technology sector, the economic success of Pittsburgh will rise. The region is once again dreaming and becoming a place where people want to move to and stay.

Though Pittsburgh is behind the country in innovation, a postmodern world has finally become a reality. Its future remains promising. Visitors see the city as a new and improved place. Miraculously, it has risen from the ashes of its economic depression to become one of the leaders in the information technology industry. As a result, it has changed overnight from a blue-collar community to a white-collar city. This change has been hard to make, yet, people are welcoming the new ideas.

Modern-day Pittsburgh

NEW KENSINGTON AND LOWER BURRELL

New Kensington is about twenty miles northeast of Pittsburgh, along the Allegheny River. Although it is in

Westmoreland County, the location along the river connects it to the city of Pittsburgh. Historically, it was called by many "The Aluminum City."

The city began the twentieth century with great opportunity and optimism. Aluminum had gone from being a precious metal to one used in everything. It was the new material for this new century and it was having a significant role in the culture and society. A considerable number of industries contributed to the growing economy of this booming city. The Allegheny Valley offered jobs in alloys, titanium, and various metals. Companies such as Alcoa, PPG, the American Window Glass, Allegheny Ludlum, and Braeburn Steel gave an unusually prosperous market to the area. Ever-expanding development gave rise to a prosperous future. Many new families were moving into the area. New homes rose out of the ground as the desire to live in this valley grew. The Allegheny Valley was the place to live and raise your children. New Kensington was "considered as the cradle of the aluminum industry."[8] It was a city rapidly growing in stature.

However, the industry that made the city great began to decline in the 1960s. "By the middle of the 1970s most of the manufacturing operations had disappeared from the New Kensington scene; one after another moved to other locations."[9] The decline of the steel and coal industry in western Pennsylvania had begun. The common scene of a blast of fiery white light from a steel furnace was noticed less and less. Western Pennsylvania, which had become the hub of industry, was in economic turmoil. The winds of change were blowing across this section of northeastern United States. Plant closings throughout western Pennsylvania sent the region into shock.

8 The Women's Club of New Kensington, *Lore of Yore: A History of New Kensington, Arnold and Lower Burrell* (New Kensington, PA: Buhl Brothers Printing, 1986), 62.

9 Ibid., 63.

Thousands of steel and coal workers found themselves jobless and depressed. In New Kensington, many companies have gone completely out of business. The business district has become a shell of its former self.

As this was occurring, the reputation of the city sank with the economy. New Kensington became known as "'Little Chicago' because of the bootleg raids, bombings and rum battles."[10] A historic pattern was developing in the community. When economic decline occurs and hopelessness prevails, negative attitudes and influences take control.

Many people saw the closing of business after business. The economic infrastructure of the city was depressed and that feeling flowed into the community and personality of the area. Unemployment prevailed and money was scarce. As the population began to decline, younger families moved to other areas of the country to find work. Those who were left behind grew helpless to reverse the trends. As a ripple-down effect, the churches were affected by this downturn. The self-esteem of the congregations fell as they watched their memberships wither. They were helpless in doing anything about this serious condition.

However, there was one city in the valley that was not as strongly affected—Lower Burrell. This next door neighbor held steady despite the economic downturn of the area. Lower Burrell was not built upon industry, but rather was the home of small businesses and department stores.[11] There were a variety of choices in this town as compared to New Kensington. Businesses, restaurants, and families began relocating to Lower Burrell. One reason was that the economy was better. An environment was created that fostered both public and private investment. Business programs were instituted to revitalize

10 Ibid., 45.

11 Ibid., 93.

the city and spur economic growth. There were many more opportunities for residents and visitors alike. Another, more serious, reason was to live in a safer, suburban area. The city was comprised primarily of middle-class white American families.

The rapid growth of Lower Burrell brought two distinct communities into existence. New Kensington was receiving a bad reputation while Lower Burrell was becoming the place to move, live, and find a quality career. Lower Burrell reflected a renewed spirit and level of confidence that had left New Kensington. It was experiencing the sprawl of expansion. There was undeveloped land waiting for growth. Therefore, not only were residents changing their opinions of the towns, churches were at a moment of truth. Would they take the challenge to move and relocate to a community that was growing? Would they stay in New Kensington and try to make the city a better place? Each congregation was wrestling with this momentous decision. It was a hard decision that Trinity United Christian Church eventually had to make. The time for doing the same things with no results was finished. Trinity United Christian Church wanted to live out the powerful life of Jesus Christ, mediated by the Holy Spirit, revealing the Father. Trinity United Christian Church wanted to thrive, not just survive. The question was, "How?" Finding the answer would require further investigation.

CHAPTER TWO

THE HISTORY OF TRINITY UNITED CHRISTIAN CHURCH

Trinity United Christian Church (TUCC) is located in the Allegheny Valley, which provides great opportunity and enormous challenges. Valley diversity, secular attractions, and cultural forces affect this church's potential for growth. TUCC does not operate in a vacuum. The pastor must understand the religious history that is ingrained in the lives of the people. Combining the economic and social forces, the leadership must fashion its strategy in such a way as to maximize the potential and avoid snares.

Trinity United Christian Church is a merger of two distinct church congregations: Trinity United Church of Christ and First Christian Church. To understand this merger, it is important to not only recognize but respect each church's distinct history. This chapter focuses on the history of these two churches and how their merger was birthed. It also looks at the new merger's (Trinity United Christian Church) pastoral leadership and growth pattern. These two factors are critical to the development of a strategic methodology for continued church growth at TUCC, which is discussed in Part Three of this book.

TRINITY UNITED CHURCH OF CHRIST

The history of Trinity United Church of Christ began at the same time that the city of New Kensington, Pennsylvania was birthed. In 1891, several farms were bought and a plan of lots was laid and called New Kensington. In June of the same year, the Burrell Improvement Company offered the first of these lots to the public. In the summer of 1892, student ministers from seminaries were commissioned by the Reformed Church to oversee the congregations in Salina, Apollo, and New Kensington. They came every three weeks and preached in a third-story hall on Fourth Avenue in New Kensington.

In 1894, Sunday school programs were organized. The morning classes were organized on June 3, 1894, with an attendance of forty-eight people, meeting above a feed store. The Sunday school became self-sustaining. However, preaching services were conducted by ministers from neighboring Reformed churches.

The congregation was officially organized December 20, 1895, with thirty-eight members. Three elders and three deacons were selected, while finance and building committees were appointed. A generous architect donated his services to the church. The church paid only for the blueprints and typewriting. The church building was dedicated on Sunday, November 29, 1896. The membership had grown to fifty-five. It was decided that the name would be *The Trinity Reformed Church of New Kensington*. The church always had plans for growth.

In 1954, a steering committee was created to plan a building program. Many churches were adding educational wings to their present buildings and Trinity wanted to do likewise. On January 15, 1958, the Educational Unit was completed and dedicated. However, in the midst of the project, in 1957, the Evangelical Reformed and the Congregational churches merged their respective denominations. The name of the church was changed to Trinity United Church of Christ. For Trinity, this was the end of one era and the beginning of another phase of its life.

In 1966, a new minister came to Trinity United Church of Christ from a Congregational Christian church background. During his ministry, several joint meetings were held with the First Christian Church, whose denominational tie was with the Congregational Church. The two churches shared Vacation Bible School, retreats, and Sunday worship services. (The history of the Trinity United Church of Christ and the First Christian Church was intertwined long before they met and merged in 1993.)

Hard economic times began to hit New Kensington, Pittsburgh and western Pennsylvania. New Kensington, which at one time was a shining jewel among the three rivers of Pittsburgh, lost businesses, families, and money. The steel and coal industries were either closing or moving elsewhere because the economy was declining. Downtown New Kensington was empty. The people were discouraged. The city's children had left the area. Buildings and houses became abandoned and forsaken. The demographics on all levels were devastating.

That Trinity needed renewal was scarcely in doubt. Its future was uncertain and unknown. Trinity had not been effective in evangelizing and bringing in new members. By 1991, morale had fallen so much that the church was forced to hire a part-time lay minister to conduct Sunday services. This Christian Church's pastor helped in the eventual merger of Trinity United Church of Christ and the First Christian Church in 1993.[12] God had not abandoned Trinity church. He had something more for these people. Trinity United Church of Christ could still appeal to a significant group of people if it would reach out to them in relevant ways.

FIRST CHRISTIAN CHURCH

On November 23, 1902, nine people met in a home on Second Avenue for a communion service. This group of Christians was entirely from one family of sisters. They had been Disciples of Christ in a Christian church elsewhere and wanted to establish a church in New Kensington. They held meetings every Sunday until January 1, 1903, when a hall was rented on Fourth Avenue and Tenth Street. Regular worship services began from this time. A meeting was held on February 25, 1904, concerning the purchase of property on Fifth Avenue. Five trustees were elected and the building was bought and converted into a temple for worship. This building was dedicated on July 17, 1904, by the president of Bethany College. Services were held in this building for twelve years.

On August 16, 1914, the congregation voted to sell the property and build a new church. Two lots on Woodmont Avenue and Locust Street were purchased and a building was placed on the land. Through the sacrificial giving of members, friends holding suppers, bazaars, and even mortgaging their homes, the church edifice was made possible. Through much hard work and volunteer labor, the church was paid off in 1945.

12 Rose Bateman and Irene Love, *Trinity United Church History*, August 1995, iv-xiii.

Renovations and additions were completed throughout the years. Likewise, progress in attendance and membership had grown. The Vacation Bible School and the youth ministry has been an asset to the church.[13]

THE MERGER

For both churches to be revitalized, their ministries needed to change. Most of the people from both churches were from traditional established church backgrounds. These churches had a centuries-old heritage that should not be lost. They were part of the historic Christian faith, but the message was not reaching the people. The challenge to build a new vision for growth was formidable. The churches were at a crossroads and key turning point. Another chapter in the life of both churches was closing. Could another story be written for the future?

In 1992, members from both churches discussed the possibility of two congregations, Trinity United Church of Christ and First Christian Church, merging to combine their resources and become one body of believers to share the faith of the Lord. Since its founding, Trinity United Church of Christ exhibited a pattern of steady growth. The congregation grew and expanded during much of the twentieth century. Yet, suddenly, within a few years, the march of increasing numbers ended. Trinity United Church of Christ had begun to experience a drastic decline in church membership. Year after year the congregation grew smaller. The striking loss of people caught the attention of the leaders. The church Consistory[14] recognized that they were not able to meet their continual financial obligations. The erosion of resources and people revealed a deeper problem. Church leaders began to

13 Ibid., ix-xv.

14 The Consistory is the official name of the church board in the United Church of Christ.

ask if Trinity would survive in the new century. It appeared to some that the church would eventually close its doors. Trinity United Church of Christ would be lost forever.

However, just a few streets away, First Christian Church had been experiencing some success in its congregation. The church became open to new people and change. Eventually, First Christian needed a larger facility to house its activities and members. Yet, Trinity used very little of its large building. The elders and leaders of both churches met and agreed that a merger could address several issues in both congregations. The churches started to hold monthly joint services in August 1992, and the elders made plans to share their church programs. During November of that same year, the congregations held listening and feedback sessions with their respective members. "The church leaders were clear with both congregations that they would continue to uphold Jesus Christ as Lord and follow the Bible as the rule of faith and practice."[15]

After sharing the Advent season together, the congregations proposed to merge. On January 31, 1993, the First Christian Church (Disciples of Christ) and Trinity United Church of Christ voted to become Trinity United Christian Church. The Consistory of the former Trinity United Church of Christ decided to resign its membership from the United Church of Christ and the new congregation became a part of the Christian Church (Disciples of Christ). The new Trinity United Christian Church (TUCC) met in the former Trinity United Church of Christ building. The first worship service with the new congregation was held on February 7, 1993, with great expectations for the future.

15 Bateman and Love, *Trinity United Church History*, xi.

In 1999, TUCC broke ground for a new future in a new town, Lower Burrell, Pennsylvania. The location projects great growth for the church. It is located just north of New Kensington, where growth and development is taking place. Daily, hundreds of cars drive by its new address on Garvers Ferry Road. Another growth factor is the facility and land. It is located on eleven acres of undeveloped property. The decor throughout the building has been updated, with a few projects remaining. The atmosphere is a more welcoming environment. However, for TUCC to make contact with the Lower Burrell community, methods such as mailings and social media will be used. Importantly, the strategy for giving the message of Jesus Christ to those living in Lower Burrell will require utilizing the relationships of the members and attendees of TUCC to bring the message of Christ to their neighbors, family, and friends.

With two congregations, having over one hundred years of shared and individual experiences, unconscious perceptions were formed. These were the thoughts and feelings that formed the structure of the two groups. The move to Lower Burrell had also changed the culture of the congregation, from an urban setting to a middle class area.

PASTORAL LEADERSHIP

Through training and experience, lay and pastoral leadership had become stronger. New leadership was needed to move to a new transition. Great potential was conceived when forward leadership took control. The pastoral staff was visionary. The elders and church leaders were goal-oriented. Leadership skills were developed in the laity. Likewise, the ability to receive constructive criticism was helpful. Leadership has been painful. It involved risks that could have been job-threatening. It has taken a great deal of personal fortitude to stand alone. In essence, the leaders have come to believe that we must set the example of living by faith. We cannot expect the people to live by faith if we, as leaders, do not.

A relevant question we have asked is, "Where should we be going?" We began with our *Mission Statement*, which proclaims:

> *The purpose of this church is to make disciples of Jesus Christ all the world, to teach them the exciting plans that the Lord has for their lives, and to commit them to actively work on behalf of the church.*[16]

First and foremost, we are to make disciples. Evangelism is primary and disciplemaking is the goal. Our biblical mandate is taken from Matthew 28:19-20, in which Jesus commands us to: "Therefore go and make disciples of all nations, baptizing them in the name of the Father and of the Son and of the Holy Spirit, and teaching them to obey everything I have commanded you." Our pastoral leadership is grounded in this belief. The motivation for all our prayers, preaching, and programs comes from Jesus' words. As the leadership made the Great Commission its foundation, Trinity United Christian Church began to focus on one priority: leading people to Christ.

The optimism brought into the church in the 1980s moved the congregation from decline to growth. Leadership is the key to growing a church. Thom S. Rainer comments, "Though such non-leadership factors as demographics, the history of the church, and the age of the church will affect growth potential, pastoral leadership may prove decisive in moving a church from non-growth to growth."[17] In order for a traditional church like TUCC to move forward, the leadership is all-important.

16 *Constitution of Trinity United Christian Church* (New Kensington, PA: 1998).

17 Thom S. Rainer, *The Book of Church Growth: History, Theology and Principles* (Nashville: Broadman Press, 1993), 186.

The pastoral leadership has influence. As C. Peter Wagner writes, "In America, the primary catalytic factor for growth in a local church is the pastor."[18] The senior minister's role of supplying enough positive influence to keep the congregation focused in a depressed economy cannot be overstated. At times it may have been the only presence in the church. TUCC has made the most of influencing members to visualize and implement the goals of the church. In western Pennsylvania, influence makes all the difference.

This leadership generated a momentum which both acknowledged the past, yet, planned for the future. As John Maxwell succinctly writes in his book, *The 21 Irrefutable Laws of Leadership*, "Leadership is influence—nothing more, nothing less."[19] The pastoral leadership at TUCC has helped to set a clear direction of where to go. This has given motivation to everything we do.

In the end, there has been a price tag. Several church leaders have been close to burnout. A great responsibility was undertaken by the pastoral and lay leadership. Being human, at times fatigue won over faith. Conflicts and quarrels brought tough times. Financial worries were constantly kept in mind. A strong commitment to a personal devotional life with God and healthy Christian relationships were essential. Church members will only respond to such leadership when genuine love and devotion is reflected to the congregation.

Thus, church growth requires strong pastoral leadership in this region of the country. Understanding the history of this church and presenting future challenges demanded change. Change was painful. Criticizing plans was easier than creating them. Innovation was not always accepted. The church moved

18 C. Peter Wagner, *Leading Your Church to Growth* (Ventura, CA: Regal Books, 1976), 60.

19 John C. Maxwell, *The 21 Irrefutable Laws of Leadership* (Nashville: Thomas Nelson, 1998), 17.

slowly for many years while attitudes and belief systems needed to be realigned. Yet, the pastor was willing to pay the price to help the church break out of its state of decline. We have learned at Trinity United Christian Church that when a pastor, led by the Holy Spirit, is willing to pay the price for using influence to lead a church to plan a strategy and establish goals, renewal can happen.

GROWTH PATTERN

Objective information on the growth patterns of churches is crucial, especially in a time of decline. Trinity United Christian Church went outside of its traditional programs to learn and implement new ideas to help the church grow. There were no simple answers. However, we discovered numerous churches where quality growth was occurring. We took courage from these resources and used many of their concepts and methods. Several areas in which the church grew were that people (1) expected God to do great things in the congregation, (2) were committed to reach seeking people, and (3) defined the theology of the church as "evangelistic." Because I carry a deep burden for reaching the lost, I have tried to incorporate this passion into the church's philosophy of ministry. This theological opinion reflects a concurrence with the present leadership of TUCC. Hence, the growth pattern of the church will eventually reflect this leadership and vision.

An often quoted verse of Scripture is Proverbs 29:18, "where there is no vision the people perish." George Barna's definition of vision is, "vision for ministry is a clear mental image of a preferable future imparted by God to his chosen servants and is based upon an accurate understanding of God, self and circumstances."[20]

20 George Barna, *The Power of Vision* (Ventura, CA: Regal Books, 1992), 28.

For pastors to achieve a goal it is necessary to have a God-given vision. Our goal is to create a momentum for growth whereas the congregation will take ownership of the vision and organizational life. They will set biblical goals and priorities. Finally, they will minister out of the focused dream and trust that has developed within the congregation. Our ultimate goal for growth at TUCC is both spiritual and numerical.

In 1985, the average church attendance at First Christian was forty people. At Trinity United Church of Christ it was even less. Very few children were involved in the weekly programs. The congregations were graying, with little hope for new life. Likewise, residing in depressed New Kensington gave the members no vision for the future.[21]

From 1985-1992, First Christian Church made incremental changes that affected growth. They began to dream again. An emphasis was placed on evangelism. New couples with young children were appearing throughout the congregation. Youth ministry was given a high profile. People were excited about coming to church again. Although the self-esteem of the community had diminished, the church was able to overcome this obstacle with great faith in God. The congregation refused to go down without a fight. It was not only a test of faith, but also a belief that hope was stronger than fear.

Growth did not come without disappointments and struggles. Finances were constantly a problem. With less income in the pockets of the people, fear and trepidation filled the hearts of many people. The people asked, "How would they pay for these new ideas? Why aren't we happy with what we have now?" In 1987, a vote was taken to relocate the church. The recommendation was turned down and faith went out the door.

21 This information was gathered in an interview with long-time members and leaders of Trinity United Christian Church.

Those who were against relocating felt that they had won, but the faith-filled believers continued to pray. They did not give up. For several years a power struggle with the leadership and congregation occurred. In the end, the perseverance of the leadership won.

As a result of the two churches merger (1993) to form Trinity United Christian Church, misunderstandings and false reports were spread. Yet, the leadership held fast to its course. The charismatic flame of the Holy Spirit came into the church through new members from Pentecostal backgrounds. Yet, Trinity United Christian Church never gave up the congregational and reformed heritages of the two former churches. The church believed that both the historic Christian faith and the new wave of God's Spirit could coexist together. It was not one or the other. God was not boxed into one way of worship. The church gained numerous new people from both sides of the aisle. The music changed. Yet, the traditions of the church could be seen all around the building.

A Saturday night service was started and a new door was opened for folks to come. Though this may not be seen as a gigantic growth rate, it was nothing short of a miracle in western Pennsylvania. Most churches were going in the opposite direction. TUCC was becoming known in the community and denomination as unique. Something different was happening and others wanted to see what was occurring.

In 1999, a bold step of faith was taken. It was the biggest we would ever make. The decision was made to relocate to Lower Burrell and build a new complex. Trinity United Christian Church did not have all the tools and resources to accomplish her dreams. This new campus, in Braeburn Heights, was a logical next step. Ground was broken in the fall and we started to build.

A miracle was rising out of the ground. Again, finances tried to dictate the outcome, but faith prevailed. Through several capital funds campaigns, the volunteer help of members, and faith in the impossible, TUCC opened the doors to a new church in the spring of 2000.

The good news is that the leaders are recognizing the factors related to growth. Members are discerning the cultural aspects that need to be addressed to move the church to new growth. It is obvious that after one hundred years, attitudes and assumptions that prohibit growth are intact. Many of those ideas have been a blessing to the church and yet, they have also been a hindrance to growth. TUCC must be committed to remaining open to the need for change or it will eventually stagnate and die. This points us toward an encouraging setting for growth in Lower Burrell.

At TUCC we want to provide Jesus' message in a form and language that today's culture can understand and embrace. We are a traditional church that is trying to relate to an ever-changing world. We desire to develop ministries that can continually adjust, adapt, and change with our changing culture. The church's goal was to move from the year 1950 to the year 2000, especially in regards to the music of today. Our goal is to come into the twenty-first century.

Change must occur. TUCC has been on a course of remapping its goals and objectives. We are feeling our way forward, navigating through uncharted waters. We are reinventing the structure of the church, seeking to engineer a new course for the future that will fit into the twenty-first century. No longer do we desire to do church as it has always been done. In an age of church shopping and lack of denominational loyalty, churches must met the needs of its constituents. People are interested in spiritual things, including Jesus. This is an unprecedented opportunity to accomplish new possibilities. God is still God, and our mandate is to serve our Creator and present the Gospel in containers from which today's people can drink. Every generation needs a shape that fits its soul to receive the living water of Jesus Christ.

Several people who have left us stated that this "new" style of church at TUCC is not their idea of a church. They have joined other congregations in New Kensington, which are still in the 1950s model of ministry. They do not see the new music, sermon techniques, and worship experiences as good or needed. Churches around the country are wrestling with this issue, but the lines are clearly drawn in Pennsylvania.

Mainline churches have tended to retain the cultural values and priorities of the past. Today's youth and young adults have come to hold the values of a new culture. Increasingly, churches have been viewed as irrelevant and stuck in the past. The challenge for our leadership has been, "How do we get people to ask new questions and think in different ways?" With all the changes occurring in this community, Trinity United Christian Church will have to work harder and smarter to reach people and relate to a new generation. Would an older congregation based on a model from the industrial revolution change to relate the Gospel of Jesus Christ to the postmodern United States? If our purpose is to lead people to Jesus Christ and make disciples, then the church's mission must motivate its vision for future growth.

PART TWO

EVANGELISM AND DISCIPLESHIP FOR CHURCH GROWTH

What is *church growth*? Is it a "numbers" game? What is its purpose? Does it have a competitive nature? What did *church growth* look like with the New Testament Church? What turn has *church growth* taken down through the centuries? What does *church growth* look like today? How does a church pursue its growth in the twenty-first century? These are some of the many questions asked today as clergy and parishioners alike pursue church growth in their individual churches and denominations.

Church growth, according to the Word of God, is not merely a "numbers" game. In fact, it isn't a game at all. It is actually a mandate from Jesus Christ, the establisher and cornerstone of the universal Church. Yet, church growth certainly involves numbers, as alluded to in Acts 2:41. The Church (*universal*) is made up of people who are counted as members of the Body of Christ. The *institutional* church—those churches comprised as various entities belonging to various denominations and those who consider themselves as non-denominational (or inter-denominational)—is also made up of people who are counted as members (though not necessarily of the Body of Christ). Jesus speaks on this when He tells the parable of the weeds (Matt. 13:24-30).

There is another side to church growth. Although numbers are important, numbers, in-and-of-themselves, do not constitute real church growth. Real church growth is internal, within the actual numbers. In other words, real church growth is achieved when each member is internally and eternally transformed by the saving Word of God through Jesus Christ. It is a *spiritual* transformation of the *numbers*. Therefore, *church growth* is both *numerical* and *spiritual*. "This growth involves a numerical increase, but it is more than that. It is the growth of each believer and the corporate growth of the church toward 'the whole measure of the fullness of Christ' (Eph. 4:13, NIV)."[22]

The first church, of two thousand years ago, was a vital and growing body, yet it had the worst demographics of any church in history. There were no high-tech marketing schemes either. However, Acts 2:41 states that three thousand people were added to the Church in one day! A larger company of people was won to Christ in one day than in the three years of Jesus' ministry. Jesus prophesied that the disciples would do greater works: "'I tell you the truth, anyone who has faith in me will do what I have been doing. He will do even greater things than these, because I am going to the Father. And I will do whatever you ask in my name, so that the Son may bring glory to the Father.'" (John 14:12, 13).

In order to adequately inspire, develop, and institute *church growth*, as Jesus mandated, the church must be involved in both *evangelism* and *discipleship*. In Matthew 28:19-20, Jesus commanded His disciples with what we call today *The Great Commission*: "Therefore go, and make disciples of all nations, baptizing them in the name of the Father and of the Son and of the Holy Spirit, and teaching them to obey everything I have commanded you." The making of disciples must begin with evangelism and follow through with discipleship. They involve baptism and teaching. Evangelism is not complete without discipleship and discipleship cannot take place without first evangelizing. It is the *evangelized* convert who is the recipient of discipleship. "Evangelism that does not lead to and include discipleship is shallow and abortive; discipleship that does not result in evangelism is ingrown and deceptive."[23]

22 Roy G. Edgemon, "Evangelism and Discipleship," *Review & Expositor* 77 (Fall 1980): 539-547.

23 Ibid., 539.

Church growth is not just an *in-ward* act of evangelism. It is not a "calling of outsiders" into the church membership from within the Sunday morning worship service. Certainly that is a means to an end, but not the end itself. Church growth involves a powerful *out-ward* act of evangelism, a making of disciples of all people. In *The Great Commission*, Jesus says "go," "make," "baptize," and "teach." Notice that these are all *action* verbs.

> Evangelism and discipleship training, or equipping, must be understood in the context of the Great Commission. Christ did not separate these two supreme tasks of the church. His words are not to be interpreted as a twofold commission of evangelism and discipleship, but rather as a single command to "make disciples."[24]

Baptism is the result of "going and making." Baptism is the end result of evangelism, when one is converted to a life and relationship with Jesus Christ. Teaching is administered to a baptized disciple, one who has "ears to hear." This is discipleship.

In this section, the I will take a close look at the biblical bases for evangelism and discipleship as the conditions for true church growth. Chapter 3 gives meaning to the Greek noun and verb that combine to form the concept of evangelism, along with its general Old and New Testaments usage and implications. I also consider evangelism as perceived in the Gospels and Acts. Lastly, I examine Paul's involvement in evangelism as well as his teachings on it.

Chapter 4 presents the biblical foundations for discipleship by first defining "disciple" and "discipleship" and how they were generally implied in the Old and New Testaments. Jesus' method of discipleship will be discussed over-against the standards of

24 Ibid., 540.

Jewish discipleship in His day. This is clearly seen throughout the Gospels. Discipleship is clearly addressed throughout Acts, from the onset of the ushering in of the Holy Spirit into the lives of the one hundred twenty in the Upper Room in Jerusalem (Acts 2:1-4) to the establishment of various "house" churches throughout the "known" world at that time. Paul's letters to the various churches are prime examples of discipleship—from apostle to believers and from believers to believers. As Paul writes to Timothy and Titus, he admonishes them to continue strong in discipleship as an integral part of their pastoral duties.

Chapter 5 develops a theology for church growth in the twenty-first century. It declares that we must first take a closer look at the post-modern era in which we live: pop culture, new age, rap, hip-hop, etc. There is a growing movement in today's generation that defies authority and lives with distrust of others who are not like them. This generation (our youth and young adults) live in a different world, one counter to that of their parents (the older generation). There must first be an understanding of the mores of these younger generations. This means, for us, "older" church members, that we must be willing to reach out to them— learn about them and learn from them. They are our future church members, if we are to have a future church. We must study the ministry of Jesus and see how He reached out and related to the "misfits" of His day. Developing a theology for church growth for the twenty-first century means first developing theologies for evangelism and discipleship. These theologies are incorporated into a postmodern era, thus mapping an adequate theology to be undertaken by the church of the twenty-first century.

In all of this, we are reminded by Kennon Callahan:

> In the coming years we need churches that are interested in success and fewer churches that are

> preoccupied with their own problems. We need more churches committed to effective mission and fewer churches caught in the web of their own shortcomings and needs. We need more churches that are planted for mission and success and fewer that are frozen in their own weaknesses and failures.[25]

In other words, God's people must realize that God, and only God, is at the heart of church growth.

Tunch Ilkin, formed player for the Pittsburgh Steelers and radio announcer came several times to Trinity for the PA Christian Church (Disciples of Christ) Tri-County Mens' Meeting when it was held in Lower Burrell. He always gave an inspiring talk, told good Steeler stories and encouraged us to leave a Christian legacy for the Lord in our lives!

25 Kennon Callahan, *Twelve Keys to an Effective Church* (San Francisco: Harper&Row, 1983), xxi.

CHAPTER THREE

THE BIBLICAL FOUNDATION FOR EVANGELISM

What is evangelism? How do we define it so that it maintains its universality down through the ages? How we define evangelism shapes how we practice evangelism.

At the 1974 International Congress of World Evangelization, which produced the Lausanne Covenant, evangelism was defined by stating, "Evangelism itself is the proclamation of the historical, biblical, Christ as Savior and Lord, with a view to persuading people to come to him personally and so be reconciled to God.... The results of evangelism include obedience to Christ, incorporation into his church and responsible service in the world."[26] However, evangelism, according to its biblical connotations, goes beyond the proclamation about Jesus the Christ. John the Baptist and Jesus the Christ were both evangelists: John proclaimed the coming of the Kingdom of God as well as the One who was to bring it. Jesus proclaimed the

26 David B. Barrett, "Evangelize! An Historical Survey of the Concept," *Global Evangelization Movement: The AD 2000 Series* (Birmingham: New Hope, 1987), 10.

coming of the Kingdom of God. He did not proclaim Himself as Savior and Lord, but as One who had been *sent* by His Father to do the work of His Father.

In order to understand the biblical foundation for evangelism, one needs to understand its concept from classical Greek literature. Since the New Testament was originally written in Greek, it makes clear sense to study the Greek words associated with the concept of evangelism.

There is no Greek word for *evangelism*. However, this English word was derived from two Greek words: *euangelion*, an adjectival noun meaning "good news" (or "gospel") and *euangelizomai*, a verb that means "to proclaim good news." Therefore, *evangelism* is "the proclamation of good news."

Evangelism is not a new concept that was introduced in the New Testament Scriptures. "The proclamation of good news" reaches far back, to the Hellenistic era. The view is the same, yet the content is different.

> The noun *euangelion* means: (a) the reward received by the messenger of victory (his good news brings relief to the recipients; therefore he is rewarded); (b) the message itself, chiefly a technical term for the message of victory, but also used of political and private messages bringing joy. Such messages are seen as a gift of the gods. . . .(c) It is chiefly in connection with oracles (i.e., the promise of some future event) and in the imperial cult that *euangelion* acquires a religious meaning.[27]

In the Old Testament, *evangelism* was associated with the announcement and publication of Yahweh's kingly rule over the world. The messenger was His prophet Isaiah, proclaiming

27 U. Becker, "Gospel, Evangelize, Evangelist," *TNIDNTT* 2: 107-112.

the good news of peace and salvation (Isa. 41:27; 52:7).[28] The prophetic messenger of glad tidings and his powerful, effective word was kept alive by Rabbinic Judaism. The Jewish hope of salvation was contingent upon the unknown messenger himself: his appearance and his act of proclamation.[29]

Throughout the New Testament, *euangelion* and *euangelizomai* are found in varying degrees. *euangelion* has become the central theme of Paul's theology, occurring quite often in his epistles. As a matter of fact, the noun is used more in the Pauline epistles than in all four Gospels put together. The verb *euangelizomai*, and its many derivatives, is used almost exclusively by Luke in both his Gospel and Acts. Mark and John make no use of the verb, and Matthew uses it only once.

Another observation with regards to the explicit mentioning of the "good news" and the "proclamation of the good news," is that neither is mentioned in John's Gospel. However, the thought expressed by John throughout his Gospel certainly has evangelical overtones. "In the Johannine writings . . . the concept is expressed by terms like *martyreo*, to witness, and *martyria*, witness."[30]

The remainder of this chapter focuses on the expressed usage of the noun *euangelion* and the verb *euangelizomai* (and its derivatives) and their implications toward evangelism in the Synoptic Gospels (Matthew, Mark, and Luke), Acts, and the Pauline epistles. What was the "good news" during Jesus ministry? How was it proclaimed and by whom? What "good news" did the early Church proclaim at its onset and throughout Paul's missionary, Gentile ministry? The answers to these questions supply the biblical foundation for evangelism.

---

28 Ibid., 108-09.

29 Ibid., 109.

30 Ibid., 110.

EVANGELISM IN THE GOSPELS

In the Synoptic Gospels, the proclamation of the "good news" or "gospel"—*evangelism*—was conducted mainly by Jesus Himself, preceded by His forerunner, John the Baptist. John the Baptist and Jesus Christ were the first true evangelists of the New Testament. Their proclamations centered around one central theme: the Kingdom of God. Matthew, Mark, Luke, and John are the four Gospel evangelists who give us the "good news" about the historical and biblical Jesus Christ: His life (for the most part), ministry, death, resurrection, and ascension.

What is the "good news" as explicitly alluded to by the Synoptic Gospel evangelists? Clearly this "good news" is the Kingdom of God and its in-breaking into salvation history (Matt. 4:23; 9:35; 24:14; 26:13; Mark 1:14, 15; Luke 4:43; 8:1; 16:16). The *good news* is that the "good news" (the "gospel") is not for a select few or the elite, but that it is to be proclaimed throughout the whole world (Matt. 24:14; 26:13; Mark 14:9; 16:15; Luke 2:10; 4:18a). The *good news* is that he who leaves his life for the "good news" will save it (Mark 8:35; 10:29). Mark begins his Gospel by proclaiming that the "good news" is about Jesus the Christ (1:1). Luke proclaims that the *good news* is "freedom for the prisoners, recovery of sight for the blind, and release from oppression" (4:18b). According to Luke, the *good news* is that in the proclamation of the Gospel "the blind receive sight, the lame walk, the leprous ones are cured, the deaf hear, the dead are raised, and the poor hear it" (7:22). The *good news* is that our sins are forgiven (Mark 2:1-12); God has already done so, by his grace and mercy towards us.

Under Jesus' proclamation of the "good news" of the Kingdom of God, people were being healed everywhere (Matt. 4:23; 9:6; 9:35). Jesus commanded His disciples to preach the "good news" (the Kingdom of God) to all creation, promising the accompaniment of various signs, such as healing, new tongues, exorcism of demons, etc. (Mark 16:15-18).

Although John does not utilize the Greek terms *euangelion* and *euangelizomai* in his Gospel, it is quite clear that he is proclaiming the "good news" of Jesus Christ and about the kingdom of God. John declares Jesus Christ as the "good news" in that God Himself has come to be one of us (fully human, yet fully divine) and to dwell among us (John 1:1-14). Jesus proclaims the Kingdom of God to Nicodemus with explicit requirements regarding its sight and entrance (John 3: 3, 5, 7b). In Jesus' "Gethsemane" prayer, according to John, He prayed for future believers, the result of the disciples' evangelistic endeavors: "I pray also for those who will believe in me through their [the disciples] message [of the Gospel of the Kingdom of God], that all of them may be one, Father, just as you are in me and I am in you. May they also be in us so that the world may believe that you have sent me" (John 17:20b-21).

What was Jesus' method of evangelism? First of all, God incarnated Himself in His Son, Jesus (John 1:1, 2, 14). Throughout the Synoptic Gospels and John, Jesus consorted with sinners as He called them to repentance.

> Jesus did not lecture people about forgiveness anymore than he lectured them about sin. By consorting with the godless he acted out God's forgiveness in his ministry and was maligned as a tax collector- and harlot-lover for his trouble. The three parables in Luke 15 were probably employed by Jesus to defend this style of evangelism and to clarify the nature of God's love for the lost. . . .

> He did not come only to consort with sinners but to call them to repentance.[31]

Jesus did not remove Himself from the people, preaching and teaching "at arms length." He dwelt among them, continually calling them to Himself. He dined with tax collectors (Matt. 9:9-13); He touched the unclean (Matt. 8:1-3); He fed the hungry (Matt. 14:13-21; Mark 6:30-44; Luke 9:10-17; John 6:1-15); He healed all who touched Him (Matt. 14:34-36). Jesus did not evangelize out of the synagogue, waiting for the crowds to come to Him at an appointed time. He traveled from city to city, walking the "neighborhoods" and "beaches," relating to those whom He called to repentance and proclaimed the "good news" of the Kingdom of God.

Throughout Matthew, Mark, and Luke, the evangelists expound on Jesus' proclamation of the Kingdom of God. Of the parables that Jesus told, most elaborated on the Kingdom of God (8): The Soils (Matt. 13:3-8; Mark 4:4-8; Luke 8:5-8); The Weeds (Matt. 13:24-30); The Mustard Seed (Matt. 13:31-32; Mark 4:30-32; Luke 13:18-19); The Yeast (Matt. 13:33; Luke 13:20-21); The Treasure (Matt 13:44); The Pearl (Matt. 13:45-46); The Fishing Net (Matt. 13:47-50); and The Growing Wheat (Mark 4:26-29). Jesus clearly wanted His audience to understand His ministry and "good news"—the ushering in of the Kingdom of God.

ACTS AND EVANGELISM

Luke's portrayal of the "gospel" as outlined in Acts has its emphasis in Jesus. It is interesting to note the occurrences of the derivatives of *euangelizo* in Acts. The context is the post-resurrection witness to Christ as believers are giving their faith. The Christians in Acts see the activity of evangelism as the

31 David E. Garland, "Evangelism in the New Testament," *Review & Expositor* 77 (Fall 1980): 461-71.

heart of mission. Although the Greek word for "gospel"/"good news"—*euangelion*—is only mentioned twice in this book (Acts 15:7; 20:24), the *proclamation* of this "good news" is evident in various instances.

> Possibly this has to do with his [Luke's] particular scheme, according to which the era of Jesus must be distinguished from the era of the church, and so to the preaching of Jesus from that of the apostles. Thus he can describe as *euangelion* the apostolic preaching (Acts 15:17; 20:24), but not the preaching of Jesus.[32]

The *good news* that Luke expounded on in Acts centers around Jesus Christ (5:42; 8:35; 11:20; 17:18). The *good news* is of the resurrection of Jesus (17:18). Paul declares in Acts 13:32, 33: "'We tell you the *good news*: What God promised our fathers he has fulfilled for us, their children, by raising up Jesus'" (emphasis mine).

Although it may seem that Luke's *good news* was only about Jesus the Christ, it is clearly evident that this *good news* included the proclamation of the Kingdom of God—Jesus' "good news." Luke declared to his disciple, Theophilos, that Jesus spoke about the Kingdom of God (Acts 1:3). Philip, the evangelist, preached about the Kingdom of God (Acts 8:12). Paul and Barnabas spoke about *entering* the Kingdom of God (Acts 14:22). Paul argued "persuasively about the Kingdom of God" (Acts 19:8); "explained and declared to them the Kingdom of God" (Acts 28:23); and "boldly and without hindrance he preached the Kingdom of God" (Acts 28:31).

> The Christians 'proclaimed the good news' of 'the Gospel', or of 'the faith'. More specifically, they proclaimed the good news about the kingdom, as Jesus

32 Becker, "Gospel, Evangelizing, Evangelist," 2:112.

> had done. But this could very easily be misunderstood in the Roman Empire. . . . So it is not surprising to find them more frequently preaching simply the person and achievement of Jesus as the good news. The one who came preaching the good news has become the content of the good news![33]

In the Gospels, Jesus was the central proclaimer of the "gospel." As was previously discussed, Jesus' method of evangelism was both incarnational and relational. So also were the evangelistic endeavors of the early Church, as witnessed in Acts. The primary methods of evangelism were witnessing (i.e., Acts 3:1-8; 9:10-18; 13:6-12; 16:29-32), preaching (i.e., Acts 2; 6:10; 8; 9:22; 13:44; 14; 18:28), teaching (i.e., Acts 5:21, 25, 28, 42: 19:8-9), and literature (i.e., Acts 17:2-3). The early, post-Pentecostal believers engaged in open-air evangelism. They witnessed on "secular ground." "Throughout Acts, Paul is portrayed proclaiming the Gospel and defending it at the same time, in the synagogue, primarily (9:22; 17:2, 17; 18:4, 19, 26, 28; 19:8), but also in the marketplace in Athens (17:17), in the School of Tyrannus (19:9), and in the house church in Troas (20:7, 9)."[34] Evangelism stemmed from personal conversations with individuals to various places, including the home.

> In Acts the Gospel was proclaimed in the Jerusalem temple (5:12-26), on street corners (2:14-36), in market places (17:17), at city gates (14:17), in lecture halls (19:9-10), in the residences of proconsuls (13:7), in a praetorium (24:24-26; 26:23-27), and in jails (16:31). The homes of believers also became vital centers for the dissemination of the Gospel (16:15; 18:3, 7; 20:7-11, 20).[35]

33 Michael Green, *Evangelism in the Early Church* (The Mount, Guildford: Inter Publishing Service Ltd., St. Nicholas House, 1995), 59.

34 Garland, "Evangelism in the New Testament," 466.

35 Ibid.

Had evangelism stayed within the confines of the synagogues and house churches, many Gentiles would not have heard the Gospel and believed. "Much of the evangelism was done by informal missionaries who, while going about their everyday tasks in society, reached Gentiles who never would have darkened the door of the synagogues to hear a sermon."[36]

Evangelism within the family unit was a significant factor in early church growth. When the head of the household was converted, it greatly impacted the rest of the household (family members as well as servants, and they too followed suit (Cornelius, Acts 10; the Philippian jailer, Acts 16:25-34). "Such homes then served as centers for prayer and worship (Acts 1:13-14; 2:46; 12:12), pastoral care and fellowship (Acts 16:40; 18:26; 20:20-21; 21:7), hospitality (Acts 16:15, 32-34; 17:5-7; 18:7; 21:8) and especially evangelism (Acts 5:42; 10:22; 16:32; 28:17-18).[37]

The most significant aspect of evangelism in the early Church was the involvement of the Holy Spirit in the lives of the believers. People not only heard the Gospel of the Kingdom of God, they witnessed it (through prophecy, speaking in tongues, healing, and the casting out of demons) by the power of the Holy Spirit in the believers. This "power evangelism" was performed by Peter (Acts 5:15-19), John (Acts 3:1-9), Stephen (Acts 6:8), Philip (Acts 8:6-7), Paul (Acts 19:11-12), and the apostles in general (2:43; 4:33; 5:12). The Holy Spirit empowered the believers to bear witness to Jesus (Acts 1:8; 5:29-31; 13:2).

EVANGELISM AND PAULINE THEOLOGY

In the epistles that Paul wrote to the already-established churches throughout the Greco-Roman world, he emphatically and

36 Ibid., 468.

37 D. S. Lim, "Evangelism in the Early Church," *DLNT*: 353-58.

constantly repeated the "good news" and his having been sent to proclaim it. The noun *euangelion* is mentioned sixty times.

> In Paul *euangelion* has become a central part of his theology. It means the familiar good news: that God has acted for the salvation (redemption) of the world in the incarnation, death, and resurrection of Jesus... However, *euangelion*, as used by Paul, does not mean only the content of what is preached, but also the act, process, and execution of the proclamation. Content and process of preaching are one. They are not separated in thought (Rom. 1:1), apart from when they are set close alongside each other (1 Cor. 9:14, 18). For in the very act of proclamation its content becomes reality, and brings about the salvation which it contains.[38]

Paul's "good news" included "the power of God for the salvation of everyone who believes" (Rom. 1:16). The "good news" is that "a righteousness of God is revealed" (Rom. 1:17). It is the "good news" that saves you (1 Cor. 15:2) and "bears fruit and grows" (Col. 1:6). It is the "good news" of your salvation (Eph. 1:13) and of peace (Eph. 6:15).

Paul consistently iterated about the "good news" of God and Christ, so much so that one would wonder if the Gospel of the Kingdom of God that Jesus Christ proclaimed somehow got replaced. However, one should realize that Paul often spoke of the Kingdom of God. He spoke of the Kingdom of God as "righteousness, peace and joy in the Holy Spirit" (Rom. 14:17) and as a matter of power (1 Cor. 4:20). On several occasions Paul iterated about inheriting the Kingdom of God (1 Cor. 6:9, 10; 15:50; Gal. 5:21). "It is called 'God's good news' time and again, and though it is never called by Paul 'the good news of

38 Becker, "Gospel, Evangelize, Evangelist," 2:111-12.

the kingdom', that may be fortuitous for he often speaks of the kingdom of God in contexts where he has just been talking of the Gospel."[39]

Another aspect of Paul's preaching that is often cited in his epistles is ownership of the Gospel. He, on more than one occasion, proclaims "his Gospel." This could be misconstrued as Paul having a gospel other than the one proclaimed by Jesus Christ. However, throughout Paul's epistles, he clearly states that he is an apostle of Jesus Christ and he boasts of the Lord and not himself. Paul's humility exhibits such an exaltation of the Gospel of Jesus the Christ that he literally takes ownership of it, spiritually.

> As the "partner of the Gospel" (1 Cor. 9:23), therefore, he could speak of "his gospel" (e.g. Rom. 16:25; 2 Cor. 4:3). By this he meant the one gospel which was preached in Jerusalem (Gal. 1:6-9; 2 Cor. 10:13-16) and which has now only broken out of the bounds of the Jewish law, and become the Gospel for the Gentiles, freed from the law (Gal. 1:16; 2:7; Rom. 1:15).[40]

Another significant aspect of Paul's evangelistic writings in the epistles is that Paul's audience was the Church, those who had accepted Jesus Christ as Lord and Savior. This is a very important factor because it clearly suggests that evangelism is not a one-time deal to convert the "heathens" of this world. Obviously, the Church needs continuous evangelism. At least Paul thought so. She needs to be constantly reminded of the "good news" of Jesus Christ and the Kingdom of God. For Paul to mention *euangelion* sixty times throughout the epistles clearly indicates our need as believers to also hear and be reminded of this "good news."

39 Green, *Evangelism in the Early Church*, 63.

40 Becker, "Gospel, Evangelize, Evangelist," 2:111-12.

CONCLUSION

The greatest example of evangelism in the Bible is the Master Himself, Jesus the Christ. His underlying message was "Repent, for the kingdom of heaven [God] is near" (Matt. 4:17; Mark 1:15). Repentance and the Kingdom of God are inseparable. It is repentance that allows one to enter into the Kingdom of God and it is the Kingdom of God that brings a repentant spirit. Jesus declared that "unless you repent, you will perish" (Luke 13:3, 5). He denounced the cities because they did not repent (Matt. 11:20). For God and the heavenly hosts, there is *joy* over *one* sinner who repents (Luke 15:7). Not only did Jesus preach and teach repentance, so did the Twelve (disciples) when He first sent them out (Mark 6:12).

Jesus' evangelism was marked by teaching and preaching about the Kingdom of God throughout all four Gospels. His parables likened the Kingdom of God to the human activities of His day so that the people could understand. Jesus also elaborated on the condition for entering the Kingdom of God. Not only was Jesus' evangelism marked by teaching and preaching, but also signs and wonders followed Him everywhere He went. He spoke healing into people's lives more than He touched them. Many were healed by just touching Him. He commanded demons and evil spirits to leave the bodies of many.

Just as Jesus preached and taught with signs and wonders following Him, during His evangelistic endeavors, so it is to be with us believers—even today, especially today. In Mark 16: 15-18, Jesus declared:

> Go into all the world and preach the good news to all creation... .And these signs will accompany those who believe: In my name they will drive out demons; they

> will speak in new tongues; they will pick up snakes with their hands; and when they drink deadly poison, it will not hurt them at all; they will place their hands on sick people, and they will get well.

The evangelists—formal and informal missionaries (apostles and other believers)—of the early Church went about preaching and teaching, with signs and wonders following them. On the day of Pentecost, the Holy Spirit descended on 120 believers and they were filled and anointed with God's power. A new and energized excitement came over them. As they went forth to preach the Gospel, the power of the Holy Spirit was transferred onto others as they laid hands on them to received this gift and for healing (Acts 4:9-22; 5:12-16; 8:7, 17; 14:9, 10; 28:7-9).

> The unique experience of the Spirit of Pentecost brought in its wake the impulse and power to be the witness they were called to be. They did not preach because they were "burdened by the needs of the world" or to perpetuate themselves, but because they were spurred by a divine compulsion expressed best by Paul, "Woe is unto me, if I do not preach the Gospel" (1 Cor. 6:16, cf. Acts 4:19-20).[41]

Another aspect of evangelism that is biblically based is its various methodologies. The four Gospel writers, evangelists in their own rights, presented the Gospel of Jesus Christ from different perspectives. The methods utilized to tell the "good news" is dependent upon whose one's audience is. Matthew, Mark, Luke, and John each had different audiences to whom they initially told the story of Jesus' Gospel. Matthew's audience was primarily Jewish. Therefore, his evangelistic message presented Jesus as the Messiah who would reign as an earthly

41 Garland, "Evangelism in the New Testament," 464.

King. It is in Matthew where one reads the most about the Kingdom of God and Kingdom living (i.e., Beatitudes and Sermon on the Mount). Mark's audience was primarily the Christians in Rome. Therefore, his evangelistic message presented Jesus as the Servant. Luke's audience was primarily Gentiles (people everywhere), thus he presented Jesus as the Savior. John's audience was primarily new Christians and seeking non-Christians. Thus, he presented Jesus as the Son of God. Likewise, in the early Church, believers were very much cognizant of who their audiences were.

> In preaching to non-Jews, they [Christians] drew on Greek literature and Stoic and Epicurean philosophies when needed (Acts 17:27-28). When speaking to the religious, especially in the religious cults, they used words like *mysterion*, *pleroma* ("fullness") and *zoe aioinois* ("eternal life"); God was the Creator and provider of all and not dependent on people's idolatrous offerings (Acts 14:15-17). To others they offered God's forgiveness (Acts 17:31; 24:25) and freedom from demons, magic and Fate (Acts 16:16-18; 27:13—28:10; cf. 1 Pet 3:22; Rev 5; 18—19).[42]

As did Jesus, the early Church preachers also called for repentance (Acts 2:38; 3:19; 8:22; 17:30; 26:20).

The early Christians were up against some real, life-threatening situations. They had no airplanes, cars, trains, or even horses (for that matter) to get them to the various places where they could explode in their evangelism quests. They did not have the technology of the Internet, fax machines, computers, social media, telephones, radio, and television as wide avenues for spreading the Gospel of Jesus Christ. They were physically

42 Lim, "Evangelism in the Early Church," 356.

persecuted and trampled on by their own people and a pagan government, yet they did not regress into hiding places; they pressed on against all physical odds. But they were prepared. They were transformed characters who stayed in fellowship and service to God and one another. They were empowered by the Holy Spirit and nurtured by each other. Today, the Church has experienced just the opposite and still lacks the power and energy of the early Church evangelists. The Church has access to all of the present technologies, as well as the freedom to worship and evangelize (at least in the Western world), yet its members *do* regress into hiding places, mainly the confines of its physical structures. "Evangelism is often shallow because believers have not been properly nurtured and are not equipped to share their faith. Lawrence Richards writes, 'We have attempted to give words to persons whose lives do not incarnate them, and to hurl them against the world.'"[43]

The Church today needs to get back to the basics of spreading God's Word, and realize that it is a team effort composed of both ministers and laity (women, men, and children). The churches today can use modern geographical tools, computers, and personal influences within the communities and the governments to win many, many people to Christ. The big questions are: Are we zealous enough, convicted enough, passionate enough, determined enough to do the work of evangelism? Do we love the Lord enough to obey the Great Commission in all its fullness.

43 Edgemon, "Evangelism and Discipleship," 545, quoting Lawrence O. Richards, *A Theology of Christian Education* (Grand Rapids: Zondervan, 1975), 55.

CHAPTER FOUR

THE BIBLICAL FOUNDATION FOR DISCIPLESHIP

> An army that spent all of its time enlisting new recruits would never win any important battles. Neither would an army that spent all of its time training its troops without ever enrolling new soldiers. Enlisting new recruits and adequate training are both essential.[44]

Why are there so many church members, yet so few disciples? What is discipleship anyway, and how does it impact evangelism? Why is discipleship so critical to church growth? How did Jesus perceive discipleship? These questions, and many more, are to be answered in this chapter.

Many churches today are stagnant in their numerical growth, but, for the most part, most churches are stagnant with respect to spiritual growth. Why is it that the church doors have become revolving doors—people come in and, shortly thereafter, they leave? Yet, others stay, clinging to traditions

44 Edgemon, "Evangelism and Discipleship," 539.

and various programs which are to their liking. Many churches have proclaimed the Gospel, of and about Jesus Christ, and stopped short of discipleship, thus losing many of its members back to the world or have them standing just outside of the Kingdom of God. Roy Edgemon expresses the relationship between evangelism and discipleship: "Evangelism is the doorway to discipleship. Each believer is a disciple (learner) and must be nurtured and helped to grow and develop in the Christian faith."[45] However, discipleship goes far beyond just being a "learner" in the Christian faith. The believer is an adherent of the Master, Jesus Christ, who is nurtured and developed in his walk with Christ. In other words, he is trained and mentored in obedience to the will of God, through the teachings of Jesus. "Evangelism is incomplete if it rushes from 'soul' to 'soul,' unconcerned whether the new convert grows, matures, and reproduces."[46]

Why did Jesus spend three years training twelve men to take the helm, along with others? Was it so that they would be more ready for heaven? Was He preparing them to go to the Cross, literally, with Him and then on to heaven? Our salvation promises us eternal life (on earth as well as in heaven), nothing else. So why study the Word of God if we are already earmarked for heaven? Well, for one, Jesus said that we would do greater works than He, promising the Holy Spirit to come and dwell in us (John 14:12, 15-20). This means that Jesus has called His disciples to do works of service, ministry. Secondly, Jesus commissioned His disciples to go and make disciples (Matt. 28:19-20. He made them disciples and then commanded them to go and make disciples. Heaven is not an *immediate* result of salvation; eternal life is. Obviously, this disciple-making is not about us as individuals, but is the mechanism by which Jesus can spread His ministry unto all nations so that the whole world

45 Ibid.

46 Donald McGavran and Win Arn, *How to Grow a Church* (Glendale, CA: G/L Publications, 1973), 164.

might be saved (John 3:17). "It is not enough to have churches filled with people who are 'ready for heaven but not for earth.'"[47] It is discipleship that leads to and furthers evangelism. It is the *spiritual* aspect of church growth.

When a baby is born, it is totally dependent on its parent(s) to feed (nurture) and help it to developmentally grow. The newborn cannot talk or walk. The newborn has to be taught values, rules, and principles at an early age in order to live in this world. Well, when a person is "born again" (from above) he becomes like a newborn baby, helpless and depending on God as well as those who helped him in the conversion, whom Jesus has called into discipleship. This "born-again" person (Christian baby) needs to be fed (nurtured) and developed to grow in the way of Christ or he will die spiritually. "If we treated newborn babies as careless as we treat newborn Christians, the mortality rates would equal the appalling mortality of church members."[48]

Although the word *discipleship* is not found in the Old and New Testaments, its concept is emphatically displayed throughout the New Testament as well as Rabbinic literature. *Discipleship* is the "process of making disciples." The object of discipleship is the disciple. What is a disciple? Well, for starters, it is defined as a learner, pupil, or someone who learns by following. However, Jesus' disciples were distinctly distinguished from the disciples of Greek philosophers and Rabbinic Judaism.

In classical literature, a disciple was considered as someone who bound himself to another for the acquisition of knowledge. (Notice that discipleship was exclusively a male endeavor.) This person was either an apprentice in a trade or a medical student of philosophy. It was considered a communal relationship,

47 Edgemon, "Evangelism and Discipleship," 542.

48 George E. Sweazey, *Effective Evangelism* (New York: Harper&Row, 1953), 206.

wherein both the teacher and the disciple were committed to the same common goal.[49]

It is quite interesting that in the Old Testament, there is no Hebrew word for *disciple*. However, in the NIV (and some other English translations) the Hebrew word for *son* has been translated as *disciple* in Isaiah 19:11). Isaiah 8:16 says, "Bind up the testimony and seal up the law *among my disciples*" (emphasis mine). But the Hebrew phrase is literally translated as "among my *taught ones*," which would, in turn, mean disciples. The reason for this lack of terminology throughout the Old Testament, as compared to Rabbinic literature and the New Testament is that the individual Israelite was considered a part of the whole of God's chosen people. There was no disciple-master relationship among men. Those who were the attendants (or "pupils") of the priest and prophets were referred to as *servants*.[50]

In Rabbinic Judaism, the disciple is someone who is concerned about the whole of Jewish tradition. This person *belongs* to his teacher and subordinates himself in a servile fashion.[51]

> Within Judaism of the first century several different types of individuals were called "disciples," . . . adherents or followers who were committed to a recognized leader, teacher or movement; relationships running the spectrum from philosophical to technical to sectarian to revolutionary.[52]

In the Hellenistic era, the general use of *mathetes* as "learner" moved to a stronger term, with more emphasis—"adherent." "The type of adherence was determined by the master, ranging from being a follower of a great thinker and master of the past

49 D. Muller, "*mathetes*—learner, pupil, disciple," *TNIDNTT* 1:484-490.

50 Ibid., 485.

51 Ibid.

52 Michael J. Wilkins, "Disciple," *DJG*: 176-182.

like Socrates, to being the pupil of a philosopher like Pythagoras, to being the devotee of a religious leader like Epicurus."[53]

In the New Testament, we read about four circles of disciples: the *disciples of John the Baptist* (Matt. 11:2; Mark 2:18; 6:29; Luke 5:33; 11:1; John 1:35, 37), the *disciples of Moses* (John 9:28), the *disciples of the Pharisees* (Matt. 22:16; Mark 2:18), and the *disciples of Jesus* (far too numerous to cite). The *disciples of John the Baptist* were considered adherents of a new movement that alienated them from those of the traditional Rabbinic schools. They are the ones who "left the status quo of Jewish society to follow the eschatological prophet John the Baptist."[54] The *disciples of Moses* are the Jews who appealed to the revealed will of God that they received through Moses, thus disputing Jesus' authority. The *disciples of the Pharisees* allude to the ones who have been formally trained in the academic Jewish institutions, likened to seminarians of our day. The *disciples of Jesus* are of an entirely different class. They are called to *serve* as disciples, *never* to reach a level of mastership. They are called to forever *follow* Jesus.

DISCIPLESHIP IN THE GOSPELS

In the Gospels, the call by Jesus Christ, to be disciples and to make disciples (discipleship), is very clear. As Jesus began His ministry, a great company of disciples followed Him (Luke 16:17; 10:1; John 6:60). In Luke 6:17, the Word states that there were the Twelve ("them"), a "great number of people," and a "large crowd of his disciples." In Luke 10:1, it is clearly evident that far more than twelve men had been following Jesus. "He [Jesus] appointed seventy-two others and sent them two by two ahead of him to every town and place where he was about

53 Ibid.

54 Ibid.

to go." John declares that after a while many of Jesus' disciples deserted Him (John 6:60-66).

Oftentimes, the evangelists distinguished between *disciples* and "the crowds." "The crowds" consisted of those who certainly followed Jesus. They were more curious than anything, not making any serious commitment to Jesus. However, "the crowds" were the object of Jesus' evangelistic ministry. It is from "the crowd" that Jesus called *disciples*, to "step out" from the crowd and truly follow Him by paying the cost and making a commitment to Him.

> The objective of Jesus' ministry among the crowd was to make them disciples. As he taught and preached to them, individuals were moved to faith and began to serve Jesus as Lord (Matt. 8:18-21; 17:14-15; 19:16-22)... . Making disciples from among the crowd was the object of Jesus' ministry in Israel (Matt. 9:35-38), and the worldwide commission he gave to his disciples before he ascended was for them to make disciples of the nations (Matt. 18:18).[55]

These *disciples* were other than the Twelve whom Jesus personally sought after and called one by one into a special relationship with Him. The Twelve are the ones whom Jesus would later ordain as apostles, the commissioned representatives of the future Church. There are instances where the reader is not sure if His disciples are referring to the Twelve or others besides "the crowds." However, there are several instances where the Twelve are explicit or directly implied (Matt. 26:18; Mark 8:10; 14:14; John 13:5-23; 18:2; 31:1-12) and there are explicit indications that Jesus had many disciples (Luke 6:17; 19:37; John 6:60, 66).

55 Ibid., 177.

Jesus' call to discipleship is "Follow me." Throughout the Gospels, Jesus admonishes people to *follow Him*. What does it mean to follow Jesus? It means to go after (or vigorously pursue) Jesus as His *disciple*. It encompasses a faithful commitment and obedience to our Lord Jesus Christ, willing to pay the cost. Jesus gives strong language of what it means to follow Him (Matt. 10:38, cf. Luke 14:27; Matt. 16:24, cf. Mark 8:34 and Luke 9:23; Matt. 19:21, cf. Mark 10:21 and Luke 18:22). The message is to *deny oneself* and *take up one's cross*—willing to sacrifice this life (leaving all, including family) for eternal life (now!) by literally following Jesus in a spiritual as well as physical manner.

The Gospel According to Matthew is a concentrated instruction guide on discipleship. Jesus' primary teachings to His disciples are found in chapters 5, 6, and 7, commonly called the *Sermon on the Mount*. Jesus begins His teachings with a lesson on humility and the abundance of blessings that will be granted as one practices such. The Beatitudes (Matt. 5:3-12) summarize the expectations for being a disciple: poor in spirit, mourning, meekness, hunger and thirst for righteousness, merciful, pure in heart, peacemaker, persecution because of righteousness, and false witness against him. Then Jesus proceeds to give several teachings on how His disciples are to conduct themselves in the world (Matt. 5—7). Jesus teaches about salt and light (figuratively), the Law, anger, lust, divorce, vows, retaliation, loving one's enemies, giving to the needy, prayer, fasting, money, worry, criticizing others, pursuing God, the way to heaven, the bearing of fruit in people's lives, and building a foundation on the Rock. This is pretty hefty teaching and is only the beginning in the discipleship process.

In chapters 8-10, Jesus exhibits the prime example of what He has just taught His disciples. In chapter 11-13, Jesus teaches about the Kingdom of God, culminating with eight Kingdom parables. He continues His teaching, all the way to the Cross. He has trained the Twelve and they (except Judas) are finally commissioned to carry on His ministry unto all nations. They are *sent* to *make disciples* of all nations, *teaching* them (new disciples) to obey everything that He has taught (commanded) them (Matt. 28:19-20).

> A number of factors point to Matthew's intention to provide in his Gospel resources for discipleship: (1) the major discourses are directed at least in part to the disciples; (2) most of the sayings directed to the disciples are in fact teachings on discipleship; (3) the disciples are portrayed in a positive yet realistic light; and (4) the disciples are *called, trained, and commissioned* [emphasis mine] to carry out their climactic mandate to "make disciples."[56]

The Gospel According to Mark portrays discipleship as servanthood. Mark paints a painfully honest picture of an incomprehensible circle of Twelve men personally called to follow Christ and promote His ministry. Mark's elaboration on the human side of discipleship reflects very much the thinking of the Church today. " The disciples do not truly comprehend the nature of Jesus' ministry or teaching, which in essence involves the way to the cross through servanthood."[57]

The centrality of Mark's portrayal of discipleship lies in Mark 8:31-33, where Jesus instructs the disciples concerning His crucifixion and resurrection. Peter took Jesus aside and began to rebuke Him for saying such things. Jesus' reply was "Get thee behind me, Satan! You do not have the mind of *the things of God*, but *the things of men*" (v. 33, emphasis mine). Presumably, the disciples continue to have in mind the things of men as they

56 Michael J. Wilkins, "Discipleship," *DJG*: 183-188.

57 Ibid., 183.

later argue about who would be the greatest in the Kingdom (9:33-35), forbidding another (not one of them) to do miracles in Jesus' name (9:38-41), and sitting on the throne with Jesus (10:35-45). Jesus uses these situations to teach His disciples about the premier goal of discipleship—*servanthood.*

The Gospel According to Luke emphasizes the way of discipleship, alluding to the cost to enter into this way. In Luke 9:57-62, Jesus reminds us of the cost to follow Him. If you follow Him, become His disciple, you must be willing to give up your livelihood—a place to lay your head (vv. 59-60). (This is not to say that true disciples become homeless people, but that if following Jesus means that you might be without a place to lay your head, then so be it.) Jesus also says that you cannot begin to follow Him and then look back; one cannot follow Him selectively (vv. 61-62). To be a true disciple of Christ takes total and serious commitment. One must be willing to abandon his own security, including home and family, for the sake of Jesus Christ (taking up one's cross).

In Luke 14:25-35, Jesus teaches on the cost of being a disciple. Jesus just doesn't say, "Come, follow me, and be my disciple." He clearly teaches that before one jumps on His "bandwagon," he needs to consider the cost. He gives two analogies to clarify His point: vv. 28-30 and vv. 31-33. Emphatically, Jesus says: "If anyone comes to me and does not hate his father and mother, his wife and children, his brothers and sisters—yes, even his own life—he cannot be my disciple. Anyone who does not carry his cross and follow me cannot be my disciple" (Luke 4:26-27). These seem like harsh words, but Jesus is putting the conditions for being His disciple right out front. However, we should not be fooled by the harsh language. Jesus does not intend for us to hate anyone, not even our enemies (Luke 6:27, 35). What Jesus is emphasizing clearly admonishes a disciple to put Him (our Lord and Savior) first and foremost, even before his own life. Jesus is saying that when one becomes a disciple his life no longer belongs to him, but to Him. One must be willing to take up his cross (as outlined in the Beatitudes) and purposefully follow Jesus. Jesus Christ comes before family, friends, one's security, and even one's own life.

Like Matthew, Luke gives a synopsis of the Beatitudes (6:20-22). However, Luke complements the Beatitudes with a series of woes for the non-disciples (6:24-26). Luke iterates, as did Matthew, on the specific teachings of Jesus: love enemies (6:27-36); criticizing others (6:37-42); bearing good fruit (6:43-45); having a foundation on the Rock (6:46-49); the cost of following him (9:51-62); the light within (11:33-36); hypocrisy (12:1-11); worry (12:22-34); and the Kingdom of God (13:18-30; 17:20-37). Luke told many of the same parables as did Matthew.

For Luke, becoming Jesus' disciple goes far beyond a career change or political attachment. It is not a "new stirring of God," but an eternal decision.[58] Jesus says, "No one who puts his hand to the plow and looks back is fit for service in the kingdom of God" (Luke 9:62).

The Gospel According to John emphasizes discipleship with respect to Jesus' teaching about the vine and the branches:

> I am the vine; you are the branches. If a man remains in me and I in him, he will bear much fruit; apart from me you can do nothing. If anyone does not remain in me, he is like a branch that is thrown away and withers; such branches are picked up, thrown into the fire and burned. If you remain in me and my words remain in you, ask whatever you wish, and it will be given you.

58 Ibid., 185.

> This is to my Father's glory, that you bear much fruit, showing yourselves to be my disciples. (John 15:5-8)

Three characteristics of a disciple are given in this passage of Scripture: (1) *remain* in Jesus' words; (2) *bear much fruit*; and (3) *glorify God.* One cannot bear much fruit unless one abides in Jesus' words. One cannot glorify God except in bearing much fruit.

A disciple *remains* in Christ. The Greek word for *remain* means that one is to abide and maintain contact for a sustained time.[59] This implies that a disciple is one who has a continual relationship with Christ; he grows in an intimacy with the Lord Jesus. It is one's relationship with Christ that affects all other relationships that he develops in life. At the beginning of John 15 (1-4), Jesus explains that the relationship that He and His disciples must have is likened to the vine and its branches—Jesus being the vine and the disciples the branches. As long as the branch has a relationship with the vine, it receives a nurturing life from the vine. Likewise, the same is true for a disciple of Christ. The disciple's means of establishing a relationship with Jesus is the Bible. As the disciple immerses himself in the Scriptures, he comes face-to-face with the Word, Jesus Christ. God speaks to the disciple through interaction with the Word; the disciple communicates back to God through prayer.

The second characteristic of a disciple, *bearing much fruit*, is a natural outgrowth of discipleship. This growth can be seen in one's living, his words and deeds. What is bearing fruit? It is soul-winning, or "making disciples of all nations" (Matt. 28:19). But this is only one aspect of bearing fruit. We bear the "fruit of the Spirit" as we exhibit "love, joy, peace, patience, kindness,

59 William F. Ardnt and F. Wilbur Gingrich. *A Greek-English Lexicon of the New Testament and Other Early Christian Literature*, 2d ed. (Chicago: University of Chicago Press, 1979), 503.

goodness, faithfulness, gentleness and self-control" (Gal. 5:22-23). Peter exemplifies bearing fruit when he says,

> Make every effort to add to your faith, goodness; and to goodness, knowledge; and to knowledge, self-control; and to self-control, perseverance; and to perseverance, godliness; and to godliness, brotherly kindness; and to brotherly kindness, love. For if you possess these qualities in increasing measure, they will keep you from being ineffective and unproductive in your knowledge of our Lord Jesus Christ (2 Pet. 5-8).

Glorifying God is a third characteristic of a disciple. When one *remains* in Jesus' words, and *bears much fruit*, he has satisfied Jesus' command in Matthew 5:16: "Let your light shine before men, that they may see your good deeds and praise your Father in heaven." A disciple is Christ-like in his daily living, glorifying God with his life.

DISCIPLESHIP IN ACTS

Discipleship begins with a community of believers, fellowshipping and sharing (Acts 2:42-47; 4:32-37). However, it is not the community of believers, in-and-of-itself, that constitutes discipleship. It is interesting to note that Luke uses both terms, *disciple* and *believers*, throughout Acts. (He never uses the term *believer* in the Gospel of Luke. Many scholars and theologians agree that Luke used these two terms interchangeably, and that a *disciple* is, in actuality, a *believer*, and vice-versa. Luke was both a physician and a historian, who paid very close attention to detail. A person of such detail, one would think, would not nonchalantly use the terms *believers* and *disciples* interchangeably. This is important to consider in the understanding of true discipleship.

In the Gospel *According to Luke*, Luke never mentions the Greek word for *believer*. He solely uses the word *disciple* for those called to follow Jesus. Why would Luke then write the sequel to his Gospel (Acts) and begin to use the term *disciple* so loosely (interchangeably with *believers*)? Every mentioning of the term *disciple* in Acts has as its Greek origin the term *mathetes*, meaning "disciple." Most instances of the term *believer* have as their Greek origin the term *adelphos*, meaning "fellow believer." However, other uses of the term "believer" have as their Greek origin the terms *agios* ("holy ones") and *pepisteukotes* (have become believers) and other derivatives of *pisteuo* (to believe). No English term *believer* has as its origin the term *mathetes* ("disciple"). In Acts 9:36-43, Luke specifically refers to Tabitha as a *disciple*; the mourners as *believers* ("holy ones").

Is a believer automatically a disciple? If so, then why didn't Jesus call "believers" and instruct the eleven apostles to go and make "believers" of all nations? Perhaps many in the crowds were "believers" but not enough to *follow* Him and become His disciples. If a *believer* is automatically a *disciple*, then why do we need discipleship attached to evangelism? Luke writes in Acts 11:26, "The *disciples* were called *Christians* first at Antioch" (emphasis mine). A *disciple* is one who truly follows Christ, as Lord, as well as Savior. A *Christian* is one who truly follows Christ, as Lord, as well as Savior. Could it be that a *believer* is not necessarily a *Christian*, unless he is a *disciple*, one who truly follows Christ?

Following Christ means obeying His commandments. Many believed in Jesus Christ (as today) but did not know the teachings of Jesus. Discipleship in Acts was concentrated in the *teachings* of the way and will of the Lord Jesus. The apostles' (including Paul) and other disciples' focus was on the Great Commission given by Jesus, "teaching them to obey everything I have commanded you" (Matt. 28:20). Throughout Acts, Luke emphasizes the teachings of Jesus (4:2; 5:17-21, 42; 11:26; 13:12; 15:35; 17:19; 18:11, 25; 20:20; 28:31).

DISCIPLESHIP IN PAULINE THEOLOGY

Although Paul never mentions the word *disciple* in any of his epistles, the concept of discipleship is very strong. The epistles written by Paul stress right (righteous) living by all who profess to follow Jesus. "Paul stressed the ethical implications of the Gospel. It is incumbent upon him to live his daily civilian life in a way that is worthy of the Gospel he professes."[60]

> Paul and Barnabas not only won many to Christ on their first missionary journey, they also nurtured the new believers and helped them to grow in their newly-found faith. In 1 Thessalonians Paul speaks of his intense evangelistic efforts in the city of Thessalonica (Ch. 1) and recounts his careful work in strengthening and equipping the believers (Ch. 2).[61]

Paul understood the importance of teaching and equipping the believers to do ministry. In Ephesians 4:11-13, Paul emphasizes the importance of discipleship. He declares in verses 7-11, that Jesus gave gifts to men (the church) in the form of apostles, prophets, evangelists, pastors, and teachers. These "gifts" were called by Jesus (and should definitely already be His disciples) to disciple—to equip the saints (believers) to do the work of

60 Green, *Evangelism in the Early Church*, 65.

61 Edgemon, "Evangelism and Discipleship," 541.

service (servanthood discipleship). Why? So that the Body of Christ will be built up (strengthened) and all of us become one in the faith and knowledge of Jesus (vv. 12b-13a). Paul says that we are not to remain infants, to be tossed to and fro by every wind of doctrine, but to "*grow up into him who is the head, that is, Christ*" (v. 15b, emphasis mine). Discipleship brings us together in love and support of one another in order that the Body may grow, the end result of evangelism.

Throughout his epistles, Paul accentuates what he surmised to the church in Ephesus. In Romans 12—16, Paul gives practical guidelines on Christian behavior, allowing the Gospel to transform our lives. In 1 Corinthians, Paul stresses the accountability side of discipleship, addressing the problems in the church through the Gospel. In 2 Corinthians, Paul addresses the church's role in administering discipline (accountability), giving, and abiding in sound doctrine, while encouraging the Corinthians. In Galatians, Paul defends the authority of the Gospel, its authenticity, superiority, and freedom. He stresses that as disciples of Christ, we are not bound by legalism and church "traditions." In Philippians, Paul addresses the true marks of discipleship: humility, self-sacrifice, unity, Christian living, and joy (in suffering, serving, believing, and giving). In Colossians, Paul stresses what we are to do as representatives of Christ—that we should make Him Lord over our lives, living Christlike. To the churches in Thessalonica, Paul emphasizes faithfulness to the Lord by living for the immanent return of Jesus Christ, working for His Kingdom.

CONCLUSION

Discipleship is the "process by which one *becomes* a disciple." Teaching is an integral part of discipleship, but we must not get bogged down in solely teaching. Discipleship *is not* the "new members" class at one's church. Discipleship is not solely Bible study, especially the way Bible studies are conducted these days. "A disciple's duty does not consist in maintaining and passing on particular teachings about Jesus. The essence of discipleship lies in the disciple's fulfillment of his duty to be a witness to his Lord in his entire life."[62] However, Bible teaching and study are integral aspects of discipleship. "Instruction in the Scriptures must be viewed as essential to the Christian mission as well as instruction in the rigid ethical requirements imposed by the acceptance of the Gospel. The call was not just to belief in Jesus but to repentance."[63]

Discipleship calls for repentance and transformation, daily. Discipleship involves one seasoned disciple mentoring another believer to become a disciple. Discipleship is an ongoing process for *all* of us, whether we are clergy or laity. "Christians are like athletes in training for a contest; like new recruits undergoing discipline and training so that they will be effective soldiers (2 Tim. 2:3-5). They are disciples who are in process of becoming like their Master (Lk. 6:40)."[64]

Recapitulating on discipleship in the Gospels, Matthew iterates, "A student is not above his teacher, nor a servant above his master. It is enough for the student to be *like* his teacher, and the servant *like* his master"(Matt. 10:24-25, emphasis mine). Discipleship is imitating one's teacher and Master as one learns and serves. Mark proclaims, "No one who has left home or

62 Muller, "*mathetes*," 490.

63 Garland, "Evangelism in the New Testament," 466.

64 Edgemon, "Evangelism and Discipleship," 543.

brothers or sisters or mother or father or children or fields for me and the Gospel will fail to receive a hundred times as much in this present age . . . and in the age to come, eternal life" (Mark 10:29-30). What we see as withholding from God, He replaces with something better. Discipleship is God's provision for a purposeful life in this present world and an eternal destiny in the presence of God. Luke dispenses the requirements of discipleship—"any of you who does not *give up everything*, he cannot be my disciple" (14:33, emphasis mine). Discipleship centers on submission and dependence. It entails a complete rearrangement of one's priorities. Our Lord Jesus must be the most important person in our lives. According to Muller, discipleship in John's Gospel no longer bounds us to an earthly Jesus. "Instead, their dwelling 'in the Word' (8:31) and 'in the Spirit' (14:15-17; 15:26f.) means that they, his disciples, remain in full fellowship with him."[65]

Paul's discipleship mandate was for the believers to imitate him as he imitated Christ. The ones who disciple, strictly adhere to the teachings of Jesus Christ, being models and examples of Jesus before those whom he/she disciples (1 Cor. 4:16-17; Phil. 3:17; 2 Thess. 3:7, 9). Paul, by equating discipleship with imitation, affirms that discipleship is the commitment to obey and submit to the lordship of Christ. In short, Paul's desire is to make disciples and have them become fully committed and responsible followers of Jesus.

Finally, discipleship involves evangelism: "Discipleship is not authentic unless it involves sharing the Gospel through word and deed to others. A person's level of commitment to and progress in discipleship can be determined by his or her concern for the unsaved and his involvement in sharing the Gospel."[66]

65 Muller, "*mathetes*," 490.

66 Edgemon, "Evangelism and Discipleship," 545.

CHAPTER FIVE

A THEOLOGY FOR CHURCH GROWTH

Over the last fifty years it has become common to speak of a church growth movement in America. Magazines, books, and journals have been published specifically for this topic. Church growth thinking arose among missiologists who desired to reach people with the Gospel. The movement is an application of sociology and evangelical theology.

Much talk about church growth lacks a theological basis. If one would ask church "leaders" about their respective church growth prospects, most would qualify them numerically. Their conversations would center around how many members are on the membership roster versus how many *active* members they have. "Church growth theorists give little or no attention to what it is to be incorporated and grounded in the kingdom of God. Their focus is on membership of the church."[67]

Theology is the study of God. The church was established by Jesus and ushered in by the Holy Spirit. It was not an establishment conjured up by humankind. Therefore, church

67 William J. Abraham, *The Logic of Evangelism* (Grand Rapids: Eerdmans, 1989), 83.

growth must have a theological basis. In other words, it must be Christ-centered (since it was Christ-established).

Church growth theology has a goal of not just bringing a quantity of people into affiliation with *a church*, but bringing them into a redemptive relationship with Christ and *the Church*. Church growth has shared with evangelicalism an emphasis on personal, individual saving faith exclusively through Christ. Thom Rainer asserts that traditional church growth theology holds to the "exclusiveness of salvation through Jesus Christ."[68] The problem with traditional church growth is that it does not fully extend beyond the initial salvation of souls. Traditional church growth "cuts evangelism off at the knees" by completely banishing true discipleship.

As previously mentioned, the core of church growth, from a theological perspective, must involve both evangelism and discipleship. Both must be carried out in their fullness. "There is a real danger that the deeper theological and spiritual issues intimately related to evangelism will be set aside in the push to find a magic wand to increase church membership."[69] Jesus was not (and still is not) interested solely in numbers. Surely He has multitudes following Him from place to place, but He was not interested in calling and solidifying multitudes to Himself. Jesus was more interested in the individual soul. Jesus called disciples—those who would follow Him in pure allegiance—from out of those multitudes. For Jesus, it was not a "body" count that was most important; it was the "souls-won" count that mattered. His evangelistic efforts were not to present a decorative gospel, but to present the Kingdom of God in its reality. His "church growth theology" meant a committed band of followers who would deny themselves and take up their crosses.

68 Rainer, *The Book of Church Growth*, 75.

69 Abraham, *The Logic of Evangelism*, 78.

> The Sermon on the Mount makes it plain that Jesus made absolute demands on his followers. Consequently, he was careful not to engage disciples on false pretenses. He did not conceal the sacrifices which would be required of them, the cross which would be theirs to bear, the cup which would be theirs to drink (Mk. 8:34-38; 10:38-39). All would-be followers were forced to think through the implications of their decision and to recognize the cost involved before taking the plunge... Jesus did not force or even coax people into yielding.[70]

A theology for church growth results in a healthy church that glorifies God, produces disciples, exercises spiritual gifts, relates positively to its environment, reproduces, incorporates newcomers, and is open to change.[71] A healthy church is one that has taken into consideration the demographic, economic, and cultural factors. This chapter addresses the components of church theology, evangelism and discipleship, in a postmodern era.

Church growth theology for the twenty-first century cannot adequately exist outside of postmodernity. Those whom we must reach for Christ are the postmodern generations of the pop, hip-hop, and bohemian subcultures. This prompts the church to develop a theology for both evangelism and discipleship that truly speaks to a postmodern world. Church growth proponents must take heed with regards to the era in which we live.

Our theology must include the present and future generations. There is a great spiritual thirst in the world today. Young people, especially, want to *feel* God, not just hear about Him. They want

---

70 Garland, "Evangelism in the New Testament," 462-63.

71 Leith Anderson, *A Church for the 21st Century* (Minneapolis: Bethany House, 1992), 129-39.

to experience the supernatural. The Church has an obligation to penetrate the postmodern world to reach people for Christ.

In its quest to grow, the church must incorporate a theology of evangelism. This theological basis for evangelizing must be rooted in the biblical practices of evangelism as set forth by Jesus, His disciples, and the Apostle Paul. "New Testament churches were characterized by a dynamic witness in the world. The church gathered as a body to worship and to be strengthened in order to go into the world with a witness."[72] The church today has lost this witnessing fervor, no longer a missiological entity. It has become docile and introverted, sucked up in programs and "annual days" and building new edifices and other kinds of godless activities.

> One of the factors which keep the church from an adequate witness in the outside world is an overconcern with self. We have become introverts, religiously speaking. . . .What we are doing, actually, is patting ourselves on the back because we think that we are pretty good Christians when we have built monuments to our own glory and the memory of God.[73]

A theology of discipleship seeks to establish and embrace true followers of Jesus the Christ. Discipleship must not compromise the conditions set forth for it by Jesus. Discipleship must include accountability, biblical training for rootedness in the Word of God, spiritual disciplines, and evangelism as its goal. "Discipleship will be outcome-based. The criteria for success will be changed lives that reflect Christian behavior rather than learning a prescribed curriculum."[74] Discipleship theology

72 Edgemon, "Evangelism and Discipleship," 543.

73 Pieter de Jong, *Evangelism and Contemporary Theology* (Nashville: Tidings, 1962), 39.

74 Anderson, *A Church for the 21st Century*, 45.

implements a Christ-centered way of life in obedience to the teachings of Jesus the Christ.

POSTMODERNISM

1 Chronicles 12:32 states that the men of Issachar understood the times and knew what Israel should do. The reign of King Saul ended in disaster. King David took control and a transition started to take place. Although David was the legitimate king, he understood the nation's allegiance to the former king while he established his own. Today, Trinity United Christian Church (TUCC) is going through changes. Could it be said of us that we understand the times and know what to do? What are the times?

Postmodernism is the name given to this new era. The challenge of the church is to move entirely with the culture or go against it, as we proclaim Jesus Christ and Him crucified. The values of our society are conforming to the postmodern presuppositions of relativism and multiple religions. There is a lack of acknowledgment of the success of Christianity in our western culture. The underpinnings of Christian foundations are stumbling in the wake of postmodernism's grip on society. Faith, morals, economics, and politics are increasingly split into partisan groups. Institutions of academia, law, and politics have been absorbed into today's cultural assumptions. Everyone agrees that we are living in a postmodern world. However, not everyone knows how to deal with this new age.

Since the eighteenth century and the epoch of the Enlightenment, the church has steadily lost influence. Today, we have moved from the enlightened period, a time that focused on human autonomy and individualism, to what many are calling the "postmodern era." We have moved from the optimism of modernity to the suspicion and mistrust of postmodernism. Our North American culture has rapidly disintegrated in the past fifty years. Our question is, "What will Christians do about this cultural phenomena?" Our congregations are vulnerable to accommodating the viruses of our culture.

The only constant in our postmodern world is change. Life slowly began to change in the last century, but accelerated after World War II as the culture became more secular. There has been more change in the previous ninety years than in the entire history of humanity. The decade of the nineties saw as much change as the previous ninety years. Human knowledge is doubling every two years.

Commitment to the traditional church structures has diminished, yet, there is an increasing hunger for spiritual fulfillment. The concept of truth has lost its effectiveness as an independent reality and has become dependent on an individual's experience or perspective. We are raising a generation that has little or no Christian memory, background, or vocabulary. Many Americans have no religious training in their background. Many may be religious, but not Christian. "We are facing the end of one era and the beginning of another. The world that many pastors prepared for is no more."[75] The five-hundred-year period of history that Martin Luther started—the era we know as the modern age, the era of the Enlightenment—has come to an end. America has become an unchurched culture.

The modern world was characterized by trust in reason, which made doubt the basic spiritual problem. The spiritual problem is no longer doubt. This culture has become secular and

75 Leonard Sweet, "Target the Trends," *Leadership* 14 (Spring 1993): 21-22.

superstitious at the same time. Our challenge in a postmodern era is to claim Christ. This is a unique moment that calls for creative strategies and skills.

The question for us is what moment in history are we going to live? God did not choose us to live in this place and time by accident. God wants our lives to make a difference in this moment of history. We need to be in touch with our postmodern culture but continue to stay in tune with the Holy Spirit. We are missionaries to this culture, which means we live as a part of the culture though it is not our home.

Effective ministry depends on understanding people and the culture. This is the world that Jesus died for, and this is the world He calls us to reach. In order to reach pre-Christians we must speak the language and use the methods that they understand. At TUCC, our goal is to keep on the cutting edge of what God wants us to do. This comes through times of reflection, prayer, and re-evaluating where our gifts and callings can be more effectively used for Christ.

Many of the established paradigms that churches operated in the past can no longer support a culture that is looking for truth outside of Christ. "The Christendom paradigm is coming apart at the seams. All the institutions and patterns of life that grew up during Christendom are having their foundations shaken."[76] By necessity, the church of this century must become more flexible, adapting to the culture that surrounds it. Essentially, the church must reinvent itself in order to carry out its mission. Effective churches in today's culture are trying new approaches to touch their communities with the Gospel. Unbelievers no longer look to the church for meaning and purpose. The church

76 Loren Meade, *The Once and Future Church: Reinventing the Congregation for a New Mission Frontier* (New York City: The Alban Institute, 1991), 25.

must change its focus. We must return to the apostolic approach of being missionaries to reach people different than us.

We are waiting for lost people to come to us. We must take the initiative and pursue the lost. We must return to the first-century model for our guidance. In a churched culture, the focus is on maintaining the status quo because people seek out the church. In an unchurched culture, we must seek out the unchurched or watch the church die. In a churched culture, evangelism is done in the church. In an unchurched culture, evangelism is done outside the four walls of the building. In the twenty-first century, most of our mission must occur in our everyday living, both to the churched and unchurched culture.

In a postmodern world, human needs are still the same. People want meaningful relationships. We must build genuine relationships with lost people. We must make strangers into friends. We need to listen to the way the culture reads and talks. Lost people matter more than our acquired comforts. It is counter to missionary activity to expect people to talk and act like us before we relate to their lives. The church must use a language the postmodernists understand. "If, in our evangelistic enterprise, we act as though a non-Christian is asked to accept along with the Christ a worldview which has become outdated, we are guilty of putting the offense of the Gospel in the wrong place.[77] Therefore, the church must change. This means less focus on our structures and more energy given to discover ways to seek the lost. The church's effectiveness in any given culture is always directly tied to its ability to share Jesus Christ and minister His love to people in meaningful ways. "An astute observer has said that there are two dangers facing the church: one is that we change the message, the other is that we

77 de Jong, *Evangelism and Contemporary Theology*, 92.

fail to change the method. Churches must realize that 'what is changeless must be fitted into a perpetually changing scene.'"[78]

> The task of theology . . . is to present the message of the church in clear and understandable terms before the people of one's day and age. Every minister must know his field, and every lay witness must be acquainted with the content of his faith. He must be able to distinguish . . . what belongs to the Christian faith and what is a distortion of it.[79]

Postmodern youth and young adults are starving for spiritual encounters. They try countless belief systems in an effort to fill the spiritual void they know exists inside them. Experience has a higher value than interpreting the Scriptures. Postmodern experience transcends former ideas of truth. The subjectivism related to experience clouds the meaning of truth. Postmodernists have no desire for a teaching magisterium like that of the Roman Catholic Church. Today, many church leaders are uncertain about the meaning of words such as "God," "Jesus," and the "Bible." Some churches believe that we cannot have absolute knowledge about God. Some are not sure there is a real and living God. Hence, if we are unsure about the nature of God and His reality, we will be ambiguous about the relevance of Scripture in a postmodern world. For a Christian who promotes that God is "the ground of our being," the reality of a personal God is meaningless. God is both real and personal. To the postmodernist, the tangible world, politics, and social justice have more reality than a personal, unseen God. Hence, the focus shifts from heavenly to earthly empirical facts. "God cannot be known in abstraction. God, in Himself, is no other than God as He meets us and speaks

78 Edgemon, "Evangelism and Discipleship," 546, quoting Sweazy, *Effective Evangelism*, 23.

79 de Jong, *Evangelism and Contemporary Theology*, 56.

through human lives of flesh and blood, lived in obedience by the members of the Body of Christ."[80]

The information age is shifting nearly every aspect of life. Our lifestyles (dress, language, values, work) shift every few years. The pace of change provides a great challenge to the Church. Society shapes the way people live, think, and believe. In an age where immorality literally flies in the faces of the world, through television, magazines, and the Internet, the Church must be careful not to allow issues of immorality divide it or stop it from evangelizing. Race, money, abortion, homosexuality, and pornography have become the mainstays of a world gone bad. These issues and the debate over gender roles in the Church have become, more so in the twenty-first century, dividing devices in the Church. For the Church to become effective in change, it must rise above these issues and target the hearts of postmodernists. The church must understand the social changes and their effect on peoples' lives and expectations. "The 21st-century church must recognize the new diversities and minister to people where they are and where they have been."[81] We must constantly consider how to organize church and ministry.

In a postmodern world, we need to think of church ministry as a cross-cultural experience. Many church conflicts occur not from personalities, but from cultural shifts. It would behoove the church to take the stance that Paul did: "To the Jews I became like a Jew, to win the Jews. . . . I have become all things to all men that I might by all means win some" (1 Cor. 9:20, 22). Hence, music and worship are not the real issues. They are symptoms of cultures in conflict.

The American church has been faced with a sudden perplexity. The United States has become the new mission field on this

80 Ibid., 109.

81 Anderson, *A Church for the 21st Century*, 32.

globe. A large percentage of our country is unchurched. "What matters is that on even the most conservative estimates there is a large configuration of groups who have yet to be reached with the Gospel and the modern church must resolutely face up to its responsibilities in this domain.[82] The unchurched people do not feel an obligation to attend a church. As secularism has invaded this country, our mission has become clear. The methods that made sense to the former generation, no longer give meaning to this new era. The local church has no choice. It must either grow in new ways to reach people or it will cease to exist. Congregations that fail to make this major change in what they do, think, and understand will become irrelevant and die.

The understanding of change must be the first priority toward accommodating church growth in a postmodern society. Renewal will come through the theology in peoples' minds, not by techniques and gimmicks. Change relates to two areas in postmodernism: authority and boundaries. Words such as "Lord," and "submission" are not in the vocabulary of a postmodern person. These concepts represent absolute authority and there is no recognition of hierarchy in a postmodernist's life. Encouraging change in the state of Pennsylvania will be a challenge, not from the perspective of a postmodern mind, but rather from a traditionalist's viewpoint. This will be a struggle and a challenge. However, this struggle must begin with the pastors and other ministers of the Church.

What are the Church's choices in a postmodern world? We can isolate ourselves from it, or accommodate it. We must contextualize our situation with the Gospel of Jesus Christ. We need to communicate the Gospel in a language that is within people's cultural concepts and ideas. The question is not whether the culture impacts the church. The real question

82 Abraham, *The Logic of Evangelism*, 75.

is will the church recognize the times and respect the culture. "Being culturally relevant is actually another way of describing what incarnating the Gospel is all about."[83]

To be effective in the postmodern era, the church must be aware of the paradigm shift which has occurred regarding leadership in the ministry. Leaders must continually redefine their structures in order to reach people. The church must be a place where learning is continually in progress. Leaders must evaluate assumptions and activities; they must understand the cultural context. An inward-focused church will not grow or learn. Each church must have an outlet to test assumptions so that church growth effectiveness can occur. In other words, people must come out of their comfort zones so that they will be alerted to the need for change.

The churches that are expanding their horizons and relating the Gospel message to this culture are increasingly living in a different world than the traditional parishes. The divisions are less pronounced by denomination or doctrine, but rather by the basic paradigm shift between those who have claimed the postmodern culture for the Gospel of Jesus and those who have not. Too many of our churches have a sign out front that matches the marquee I noticed in an antique store in Pennsylvania that says, "Walk back into the past with us!" Yet, this is the paradox of the postmodern church. The enduring message of Jesus is the core of the congregation, yet, the appearance looks like the twenty-first century; they are just not yet there. Our Lord Jesus commanded, "Therefore, go and make disciples of all nations" (Matt. 28:19), but He did not tell us how to do it. He told us to preach, teach, and heal (Mark 15:17-18), but He did not give us the methodology. The postmodern church must embrace the ancient message of Jesus Christ, yet utilize the modern ideas of

---

83 Robert Logan, *Beyond Church Growth*, (Old Tappan, NJ: Revell, 1989), 69.

humankind. "This is the genius of the Scriptures. They set men free to create unique approaches and devise methods that are workable at any time in history."[84]

A THEOLOGY OF EVANGELISM

An evangelism theology must be Christ-centered, through and through. It must capture the essence of God's salvific plan to reconcile us (the world) to Him. "A theology of evangelism must show how the message of reconciliation grows out of the event of reconciliation and why therefore the death of this one man is a message which the whole world must hear."[85] It is an excursus of all that God has done through the revelation of His Word, encompassing the entire scope of Scripture, both the Old and New Testaments. "It is the language to share the outgoing love of God which alone can make life full and give it roots in an age of rootlessness. It aims at true community."[86]

A theology of evangelism must address, first and foremost, the proclamation of Jesus' gospel—to repent, for the Kingdom of God is near. Why would Jesus call the world into repentance? The world has turned away from God in sin. Jesus calls us to repent—to have a change of mind, heart, and will from this world, and turn to God by entering into His Kingdom. "Evangelism strikes at the heart of sin. A theology which does not come to grips with this cause of all human woe, individually and collectively, is irrelevant to the world's needs."[87]

In all of its magnitude, a theology of evangelism must not get caught up in church traditions, excluding those on the

84 Gene A. Getz, *Sharpening the Focus of the Church* (Chicago: Moody Press, 1974), 48.

85 Bernard L. Ramm, "The Theology of Evangelism," in *Occasional Papers*, eds. Darrel L. Guder and James R. Oraker (Colorado Springs: Institute of Youth Ministries, 1978), 154.

86 de Jong, *Evangelism and Contemporary Theology*, 111.

87 Robert E. Coleman. "Theology of Evangelism," *Review & Expositor* 77 (Fall 1980): 473-81.

inside from hearing and understanding the depth of Christ's Gospel. It must not show selectivism with regards to who outside the "church tradition" gets to hear and understand the proclamation of the Gospel, because of fears and misplaced assumptions and attitudes.

> The saving magnitude of the Word carries an urgency that it be told to every creature. From this mandate issues a theology immediately related to the propagation of the Gospel. It does not rest upon a few isolated texts of Scripture nor any particular church tradition; rather, drawing upon the whole of Scripture . . . it focuses the purpose of all that God has revealed. In this case, evangelism is the measure by which any Christian doctrine must be validated.[88]

A theology of evangelism, to be effective, must include certain components. Evangelism must be defined in its proper context. It is more than a mere definition of "proclaiming the Gospel." But that gospel is to be proclaimed in the truth of what it really is. Boundaries of evangelism must be set in place. Who's responsibility is it to evangelize and what exactly are the responsibilities of evangelism? A theology of evangelism must engage dialogue. One can understand the Gospel and take responsibility to evangelize, to proclaim the fullness of the Gospel. But if we cannot communicate it in a context that can be digested by this postmodern world, then what good are our efforts? A theology of evangelism cannot convey that those of us who are in Christ know and understand all and that the world is crazy! We must be willing to engage the world in dialogue, asking the hard questions to them and allowing them to ask us the hard questions.

88 Ibid., 474.

THE MEANING AND CONTENT OF EVANGELISM

Bernard Ramm wrote:

> Only God can make a Christian. People cannot be talked into being Christians; they can only be born into being Christians. No evangelist can justify a sinner; only God justifies sinners by faith. We may convert people to Christianity but only the Holy Spirit can make them new creatures in Christ.[89]

So what are we to do? How are we to evangelize? Or better yet, what should be our context for evangelism. Our main concern is to bring the "good news" to the world. The recipients of this "good news" are all who have not been "born again." Many have heard the Gospel and have even been baptized. But they have not been "born again." As we engage in evangelism, we must not get caught up in results. In doing what God has called us to do, we must trust Him with the results. In other words, the results are *His* business. It is the Holy Spirit who convicts and converts, not us. J. I. Packer sums it up quite nicely: "The way to tell whether in fact you are evangelizing is not to ask whether conversions are known to have resulted from your witness. It is to ask whether you are faithfully making known the Gospel message."[90] When one proclaims the Gospel to another, there is no guarantee that the person will accept it right then and there. The person to whom one proclaims the Gospel may have to hear it again and again, and from someone else. I'm reminded of what Paul alludes to in his letter to the church in Corinth: one plants the seed, another comes along and waters it, but God gives the increase (1 Cor. 3:6). J. C. Holkendijk tells us, "to sow and wait in respectful humility and in expectant hope."[91]

89 Ramm, "The Theology of Evangelism," 154.

90 J. I. Packer, *Evangelism and the Sovereignty of God* (Downers Grove: InterVarsity, 1961), 41.

91 Johannes C. Holkendijk, *The Church Inside Out*, ed. L. A. Hoedemaker and Pieter Tijmes, trans. Isaac C. Rottenberg (Philadelphia: Westminister, 1966), 21.

A theology of evangelism must include three factors: the Kingdom of God, the event and message of reconciliation, and the crucifixion and resurrection of Jesus the Christ. Those three factors are historically and spiritually intertwined. The Kingdom of God "is near" is the beginning of the event of reconciliation. This event marks God in Christ reconciling the world to Himself (2 Cor. 5:19b). God was in Christ in that "In the beginning was the Word, and the Word was with God, and the Word was God" (John 1:1) and that "The Word became flesh and made his dwelling among us" (John 1:14), the Word being Christ. Christ's coming was to reconcile the whole world to God by becoming a sacrificial sin offering (John 3:16, 17), to pay a debt to God that no human being alone could pay. "God made Him who had no sin to be sin for us, so that in him we might become the righteousness of God." (2 Cor. 5:21). Christ became a ransom to free the world from sin (Mark 10:45; Heb. 9:15). "The ground of reconciliation is then the sacrificial death of Christ in the analogy of the Old Testament Levitical sacrificial system."[92] In 1 Corinthians 5:1-8, Paul states the Gospel in the context of Christ crucified and resurrected. He explains that Christ not only died for our sins, but that He was actually buried (for three days) and was then resurrected, appearing to the Twelve, as well as more than five hundred people. Paul goes on to iterate the importance of the resurrection, the root and grounding of our faith (vv. 12-23).

The content of our evangelism must include the Kingdom of God as proclaimed by Jesus the Christ throughout the Gospels. The Kingdom of God is the rule of God in history. It is the *core* of Jesus' ministry in that it is what He exclusively proclaimed. "Any vision of evangelism that ignores the kingdom of God, or relegates it to a position of secondary importance, or fails to wrestle thoroughly with its content is destined at the outset to

92 Ramm, "The Theology of Evangelism," 161.

fail."[93] The centrality of evangelism is that people become firmly rooted within this rule—that they enter into this Kingdom—in order that they may be the disciples whom God has called, in the ministry of reconciliation. It is through entering the Kingdom of God that individuals are reconciled to God.

Evangelism involves the ministry of reconciliation, proclaiming to the world that "God was reconciling the world to himself in Christ, not counting men's sins against them" (2 Cor. 5:19a). As disciples of Christ, we are also Christ's ambassadors—God making His appeal through us—committed to proclaim this aforementioned message of reconciliation (2 Cor. 5:19b-20).

THE BOUNDARIES OF EVANGELISM

So many of God's people fill the church pews having an attitude that outright evangelism is the responsibility of the pastor and other clergy, and that their witness is limited to how they live. Both assertions are utterly wrong. As was demonstrated in the above paragraphs, true Christians (disciples of Christ) are ministers of the message of reconciliation. Every member of the Body of Christ has an obligation to evangelize. Surely, Jesus has called some to be *evangelists*, but that calling, just as that of pastor, teacher, apostle, and prophet, is to "prepare God's people for works of service, so that the body of Christ may be built up until we all reach unity in the faith and in the knowledge of the Son of God and become mature, attaining to the whole measure of the fullness of Christ" (Eph. 4:11-13). "When this is forgotten, as is often the case, the potential work force of the church flounders in inertia. This becomes most tragic in evangelism, for unless the Gospel message gets out, bringing forth new believers, how can the church be perpetuated."[94]

93 Abraham, *The Logic of Evangelism*, 17.

94 Coleman, "Theology of Evangelism," 478.

Our responsibility in evangelism is to raise the same question that Jesus raised on the Cross: "My God, my God, why have you forsaken me?" (Matt. 27:46). Why did Jesus cry out like this? Because He was at the borderline of His life. How so? Notice how, for the very first time, He only called God, God, instead of Father. Jesus was made a sin offering upon that cross, which means that He actually 'ingested' the sins (past, present, and future) of this world. God could no longer be Father because the Father cannot tolerate sin. Therefore, God the Father looked away from His Son. But God was still there (evidenced by the resurrection). And the same way He was with Jesus in His abandonment on the cross, so we must proclaim to the world that God is with us in our abandonment, waiting to become our Father.

> Fewer and fewer people ask the question and when, if they ask it at all, they will likely do so in situations at the borderline of life. If we act as though this is the only opportune moment for evangelism to take hold of things, we are giving in to a misconception, namely, that faith is relevant only when man is at his wit's end. The Gospel has something to say in the midst of life and not just at the fringes.[95]

In a postmodern context, we must learn to evangelize outside of a religious setting. Evangelism cannot be done in the context of getting people to come to church. The church cannot impose all sorts of stringent rules on people as a welcome mat into the church. We who evangelize must capture the language and culture of our target audience. We must "incarnate" ourselves by dwelling among them, standing at their sides, in solidarity with them. We must communicate with them in a way that they have a chance to react to the message and not to us. We

95 de Jong, *Evangelism and Contemporary Theology*, 38.

must throw our assumptions out the window. Postmodernists are on a totally different "wavelength" than those comprising the traditional church today. We must seek them out and learn who they really are.

> We cannot assume that people are familiar with Scripture or basic biblical ideas. We cannot assume that they feel accountable in any way to a supreme being. We cannot assume that they feel much real guilt for sin. We cannot assume that they even think at all in terms of sin. We cannot assume that they will need to have any logical consistency or coherence to their ideas about God. After all, the postmodern assumption is that we create our own reality in the arena of spirituality.[96]

The boundaries of evangelism must extend beyond the proclamation, to include one's initiation into the Kingdom of God.[97] What the institutional church does is initiate new converts into its institutional structure, ignoring the Kingdom of God altogether. To what avail is this done? The church does not have the power to keep a new convert within its premises. However, initiation into the Kingdom of God empowers the new convert to truly follow Christ and become His disciple. Evangelism is about "cut-throat" repentance on the part of the believer. It is more than getting a confession by mouth and the repeating of a "Sinner's Prayer." God wants every believer to believe enough to trust in the sovereign rule of God, not the rules of the denomination. "Entry into the Kingdom of God is not a casual affair. It involves a radical confrontation with God, and it seems impossible that it could happen without a profound self-examination and penetrating self-knowledge."[98] Abraham's approach is for evangelism to extend its role beyond

96 Rick Richardson, *Evangelism Outside the Box: New Ways to Help People Experience the Good News* (Downers Grove: InterVarsity, 2000), 122.

97 Abraham, *The Logic of Evangelism*, 97.

98 Ibid., 121.

the mere proclamation of Jesus Christ to get the real Gospel out, the arrival of the Kingdom of God, which can be actualized in the hearts and lives of humankind through Jesus the Christ.

Effective Evangelism through Dialogue

One of the most critical components of effective evangelism is caring communication. What good is the Gospel if it cannot be effectively communicated to those who are lost in sin? Communication must be a two-way effort. In other words, evangelism must engage in dialogue, between the one evangelizing and the one being evangelized. Dialogue must be engaged in a respectful way, with compassion and a genuine interest in the person with whom you are speaking. Jesus has called us to be disciples in order that God could communicate the faith, the Word, and the Gospel through us. However, we must remain cognizant that the Holy Spirit is the *final* agent in the communication. The Holy Spirit is the One who checks the heart of the hearer and decides whether the bearer of the "good news" will connect with the hearer. "The man who is addressed by the Christian is able to listen and understand to a certain extent what he is saying. It makes sense, but only God can bring it to life so that it "lives" for him and true community is born, both between the partners in conversation and between them and God."[99]

In our communication of the Gospel with others, we must be sensitive to the other person's culture, lifestyle, and possibly his religion. We must look beyond the outer appearances of those whom we seek to hear the Gospel. We must be willing to engage in dialogue with the homeless, the gangbanger, the person with body piercing, and the person whose hair style/ color is "outrageous" in our eyes. We must dispense of our

99 de Jong, *Evangelism and Contemporary Theology*, 58.

predisposed attitudes and remember that every human being was created by God and therefore, is a soul that needs salvation. Many of us must look at ourselves and where we came from in order that we will not misjudge others. But the fact of the matter is that evangelism is not about the Christian, per se, who is doing it. It is about the recipient of the "good news." We must also be willing to engage in dialogue the "intellectuals" of our society—those who are educated and occupying the various professions of our day.

Engaging in dialogue with others requires more than a knowledge of the Gospel and the Word of God. The evangelist must know something about his target audience. Evangelizing postmodernists requires one to know what postmodernism is as well as its attributes. Evangelizing African-American youth requires one to understand the hip-hop movement. Evangelizing Muslims requires one to understand the Muslim religion and to be familiar with the Qur'an. Why is this so important? Because, like Jesus, Paul, and so many others, we want to meet people where they are. We need a point of contact. Jesus is our prime example of how to meet people where they are and engage them in dialogue.

In John 4:4-30, Jesus engages in dialogue with a Samaritan women (a "no-no" in His day) about "living water" that will truly quench her thirst. (The point of contact was the well that the woman approached to obtain water, where Jesus rested.) The woman responds in dialogue about the rift between Jews and Samaritans. Jesus then tells her about the true worshippers who will worship God in spirit and in truth. Here we have Jesus "stepping outside the box" of Jewish law and custom in order that another may receive eternal life.

In Luke 10:25-37, Jesus engages in dialogue with a lawyer who challenges Him about the law. When the lawyer asks Jesus, "And who is my neighbor?" (v. 29), Jesus proceeds to respond with the parable of the Good Samaritan. Jesus then asks the lawyer a question, and he responds to Jesus' satisfaction. In this episodic dialogue, Jesus does not commence to tell the lawyer about the law. He responds with questions that get to the root of the lawyer's intentions until the lawyer seeks to know something of grave importance to the Kingdom.

In John 3:1-21, Jesus engages in dialogue with a respected Rabbi, Nicodemus. Nicodemus seeks out Jesus and acknowledges who He is. Jesus responds with a profound statement about the Kingdom of God, which perplexes Nicodemus and prompts him to ask questions.

Other examples of dialoguing with people where they are, are in Acts: Paul at a meeting with the Greek philosophers (Acts 17:15-34) and Philip with the Ethiopian eunuch (Acts 8:26-35). In each of these instances, the evangelist made a point of contact and began to ask questions.

When we engage in dialogue with others about the Gospel, we must be clear and concise, ensuring that our hearers will understand. Our language must be *their* language. And we must do so without compromising the Gospel. In our evangelism, we must be very careful with the vocabulary that we choose. Words such as "sin," "repent," "justified," "righteous," "redemption," "atonement," and "Lord" would be foreign to most people. To approach someone with a line like, "If you should die today, do you know where you will spend eternity?" is asking for rejection of the Gospel. The kind of responses one may give in this postmodern era would probably be anger or unbelief or "nowhere." Then again, many will say "heaven" and really believe it, while they are headed straight for hell.

Our point-of-contact questions should initiate sound dialogue in order that we may give the true Gospel to as many as will receive it. According to John R. Stott, true dialogue is marked by *authenticity* ("If we do nothing but proclaim the Gospel to people from a distance, our personal authenticity is bound to be suspect."), *humility* ("We have to recognize humbly that some of his misconceptions may be our fault."), *integrity*, and *sensitivity* ("It is impossible to evangelize by fixed formulae.").[100]

A theology of evangelism sacrifices quantity for the sake of quality. Although Jesus spoke to thousands of people in His evangelistic journey of three years, He did not compromise the Kingdom of God. Jesus flatly gave the conditions to become His disciple and enter into the sovereign rule of God, no exceptions. He knew from the beginning that He would not get the quantity that He would like to have gotten. There are no quick fixes in quality evangelism. The world has changed immensely and is rapidly changing right before our eyes.

> For too long churches have yearned for a microwave solution to problems in this area. Various schemes, campaigns, programs, and other paraphernalia have been cooked up to save the world, and we have grown weary from the false hopes they have fostered. The time is ripe to set these aside and regain the patience of God in establishing God's love on earth.[101]

The church must be patient and mindful that God has not abandoned us, but wants us to engage Him and His will, that He may engage us as we engage the world.

100 John R. Stott, *Christian Mission in the World* (Downers Grove: InterVarsity, 1976), 71-73.

101 Abraham, *The Logic of Evangelism*, 112.

The church and evangelism ministry must clearly understand the true Gospel of Jesus Christ in light of the *Great Commission*. The church must seek to develop evangelism ministries that will truly embark on a mission to properly bring people to Christ and into the Kingdom of God. There must be ample biblical teaching about the Kingdom of God, why God became man (the event and message of reconciliation), and the death and resurrection of Jesus Christ. These teachings will not only convict those who evangelize but will help them immensely in their evangelistic efforts, both before and after conversion takes place. One cannot initiate anyone into the Kingdom of God unless he has entered into it. Evangelism is an "eyes wide open" endeavor.

Jesus says, in John 15:4, "Remain in me and I will remain in you. No branch can bear fruit by itself; it must remain in the vine." He goes on to say, "If you remain in me and my words remain in you, ask whatever you wish, and it will be given you. This is to my Father's glory, that you bear much fruit, showing yourselves to be my disciples." (vv. 7-8). As we remain in Jesus and His words remain in us, we are empowered by the Holy Spirit to evangelize in such a way as to present Jesus as real and as God before humankind. As in Acts, with Peter, John, Steven, Philip, Paul, and so many others, we must be under the powerful anointing of the Holy Spirit in our evangelism. To embark on such a serious venture without the unction of the Holy Spirit is like going on the battlefield without weapons. For when we engage in evangelism, we are engaging in spiritual warfare—in a battle with the powers of darkness to rescue their prisoners. "Just as the various authors of the New Testament expressed the call to faith in very different and even contradictory ways, so the modern evangelist should trust the Holy Spirit to lead him or her to achieve the same end in the modern world."[102]

102 Ibid., 126.

A theology of evangelism must evolve in the context of a postmodern era. Postmodernists are looking for a real truth and spirituality that resonate in their lives. They are looking for a community in which they can have a sense of belonging. The church must first provide this community before they can achieve hearers for the proclamation of the Gospel. "As we challenge the postmodern mindset, we need first to use postmodern rules of truth."[103] It is imperative that we meet people where they are, i.e., circumstances in life, cultures, ethnicities, economic levels, and various religious orientations. "Evangelistic endeavors that are effective in today's world will be marked with an understanding of the principles that govern a pluralistic society. *Acceptance of diversity. Appreciation of options. Interaction with alternatives.*"[104]

Evangelism and church growth are not synonymous terms. However, evangelism is a constituent of church growth, just as discipleship is. Abraham writes:

> Clearly, evangelism and church growth are not exactly identical. However, they are intimately connected in at least three ways. First, evangelism ideally should lead to the numerical growth of the church. Second, many today think of evangelism fundamentally in terms of the growth of the church. Enough confusion exists to allow many to treat evangelism as church growth without making a critical examination. Finally, exponents of the church growth tradition characteristically have been driven to reject the conventional understanding of evangelism and develop their own.[105]

103 Richardson, *Evangelism Outside the Box*, 93.

104 Donald Posterski, *Reinventing Evangelism: New Strategies for Presenting Christ in Today's World* (Downers Grove: InterVarsity, 1989), 168.

105 Abraham, *The Logic of Evangelism*, 71.

If the church would adopt a theology of evangelism that is biblically based, then numbers would not be such a big issue. If we follow the examples of Jesus and His disciples/apostles, then we can successfully evangelize in this postmodern world. First, the church must be willing to change its paradigm for doing ministry, including "church." When we obey the will and teachings of God with qualitative and effective evangelism, *He* will add to our numbers daily, those who are being saved (Acts 2:47b).

A THEOLOGY OF DISCIPLESHIP

Evangelism must lead to an active development of believers, equipped with God's gifts in order to truly follow Christ. This active development is called *discipleship*. Discipleship overlaps evangelism during the initiation into the Kingdom of God. Entry into the Kingdom is absolutely necessary for discipleship to be successful. Another component of Kingdom initiation is being baptized (or "filled") with the Holy Spirit. Before ascending to heaven, Jesus told His disciples to wait patiently in Jerusalem, for they would receive power when the Holy Spirit comes on them, the gift that the Father had promised (Acts 1:4-5, 8).

Discipleship must be properly defined, according to the teachings mandated in Scripture. Discipleship is *not* a membership class of the church. The churches have too many *different* doctrines, none of which encompasses the whole of what Jesus taught. There is nothing wrong with membership classes to cover the denominational doctrines of the church, but this is clearly *not* discipleship. Discipleship is *not* a variety menu set up by churches, wherein members can select the 'entrees' that are most appetizing to them. Discipleship is *not* Bible study, although Bible study is involved. Discipleship is *not* a program that last six months, a year, or two years. Discipleship is *a lifetime process of individual and collective growth in the church.*

A theology of discipleship sustains and nurtures believers, that they would conform to the character of Christ. This theology equips believers for spiritual warfare, ministry (to serve the church community and make disciples), and evangelism. It establishes a mentorship, wherein the student and the teacher become partners in her/his spiritual growth. Just as Jesus walked alongside His disciples, as mature disciples, we too must walk alongside (in solidarity with) infant disciples, raising them into maturity in the likeness of Christ.

Sharing their faith, and discipleship is the foundation of Trinity's youth ministry E.P.I.C. (Everyone Perfected in Christ)

THE MEANING AND CONTEXT OF DISCIPLESHIP

Discipleship makes believers into true followers of Christ. It is a necessary component of spiritual growth. It is comparable to the raising of a new born infant into a mature adult. And even as adults, we are still maturing. Therefore, discipleship is an ongoing, life-long process of spiritual growth through supernatural guidance from the Holy Spirit. In Matthew 5—7, Jesus holds "revival services" on a mountainside near Capernaum. Thus, the name was given, *Sermon on the Mount.* The *Sermon on the Mount* is for disciples (Matt. 5:1). Jesus begins His sermon with the Beatitudes. The Beatitudes are a code of ethics for the disciples. In this code of ethics, Jesus outlines the expectations for being a disciple: poor in spirit, mourning, meekness, hunger and thirsting after righteousness, merciful, pure in heart, peacemaker, persecution. However, Jesus assures abundant blessings for those who adhere to this code of ethics. Each one of these codes must be clearly interpreted to the disciples of our day, in a context which they can understand.

Discipleship is not an easy undertaking because it stands over against society's way of living. So many in our churches today are not disciples, simply because they find Jesus' code of ethics to difficult to follow in the midst of everyday life. The ways of the world seem to be far more appealing to many church-goers than Jesus' code of ethics and the *Sermon on the Mount.* However, we must remember that our goal is to become like Christ. Discipleship involves releasing our pride and independence (individualism) in exchange for total dependence on God. It involves exchanging selfishness and lust for power, humility, and self-sacrifice. This undertaking must begin with those whom Jesus has called and given authority to as gifts to the Church: *apostles*, *prophets*, *evangelists*, *pastors*, and *teachers.* We are to be the prime examples as carriers of this code of ethics.

In its discipleship training the church must be very careful and sensitive not to make Kingdom living impossible for some because of their past. We must ask the hard questions about matters such as divorce, marriage, adultery, revenge, murder, etc., and seek guidance from the Holy Spirit on how to tread in such murky waters. Remember, God has fully pardoned the past sins of a converted/*born-again* soul. It is as if that person's past does not exist, and that is how we must treat it. We must approach God's Word spiritually on a case-by-case basis, or we may so offend the convert and lose him before he gets started in his walk with Christ.

Matthew 5—7 is only the beginning of discipleship. However, this beginning is critical to Christian maturation. It would be impossible to adhere to all that Jesus teaches without entrance into the Kingdom of God and the baptism of the Holy Spirit. That is why, in John 3:5, Jesus tells Nicodemus, "I tell you the truth, no one can enter the kingdom of God unless he is born of water and the Spirit." Paul continues in the discipleship training process in his letters to the various local churches that he planted and visited. Paul talks about the gifts of God and the fruit of the Spirit.

In his letter to the Church in Rome, which Paul neither planted nor visited, Paul discusses God's righteous judgment and His faithfulness, forgiveness of sin, freedom from sin in that we are dead to sin and alive in Christ, and so much more. To the church in Corinth, Paul lashes out at those who have not grown in Christ, by calling them mere infants. He says, "I gave you milk, not solid food, for you were not yet ready for it. Indeed, you are still not ready. *You are still worldly.* For since there is jealousy and quarreling among you, are you not worldly? Are you not acting like mere men?" (1 Cor. 3:1-3, emphasis mine). Disciples are not worldly, but delight themselves in the will of God. In 1 Corinthians 14:20, Paul admonishes the Corinthian believers to think like adults and be infants when it comes to evil, the sign of a mature disciples. To the church in Galatia, Paul explains liberty from the law as one is led by the Spirit. He says that the sinful nature and the Spirit are in conflict with each other. He warns that those who live by the acts of the sinful nature will not inherit the Kingdom of God. As we are led by the Spirit, the fruit that we will bear is love, joy, peace, patience, kindness, goodness, faithfulness, gentleness, and self-control (Gal. 5:17-23). He goes on to say that "those who belong in Christ Jesus have crucified the sinful nature with its passions and desires" (v. 24).

Other epistles speak to the mature person in Christ. The writer of Hebrews advocates growth (maturity) for the true disciple. When one is truly wanting to learn of the teachings of Jesus and lives in obedience to those teachings, he will most certainly mature. The Hebrew writer expresses his or her disappointment in the believers' lack of progress in discipleship.

> In fact, though by this time you ought to be teachers, you need someone to teach you the *elementary* truths of God's word all over again. You need milk, not solid food! Anyone who lives on milk, being still an infant, is not acquainted with the teaching about righteousness. But solid food is for the mature, who by *constant use* have trained themselves to distinguish good from evil. (Hebrews 5:12-14, emphasis mine)

Peter admonishes the Jewish Christians to rid themselves of all evil doing and crave spiritual milk like newborn infants, so that they may *grow up* in their salvation (1 Pet. 2:1-2). Far too often churches have *one* Bible study session a week without any regard for discipleship. How can children of God, at various spiritual ages, all be fed the same food and survive? Has the church ever observed a mother with her newborn infant? She wouldn't dare give her Gerber or Beechnut baby food in the first three months of that baby's life. She feeds her infant child milk! The church must first feed her infant children milk!

Then, gradually advance them to baby food and then on to solid food. Many of these infants and small children stumble and fall by the wayside. Some even die because they have not been properly nourished.

A theology of discipleship demands proper teaching of the Word of God. It ensures that everyone *start off* with spiritual milk and *advance* to solid food as they grow in the Word. There must be incremental Bible studies so that each person can ingest and digest the Word of God, thoroughly, at his level of maturity.

The Hebrew writer reminds us that the purpose of discipleship is for disciples to make disciples: "By this time you ought to be teachers" (5:12). Stagnation is not a quality of discipleship. Bible study, in-and-of-itself, does not impact spiritual growth unless it is formational. Bible study must be engineered in such a way that the Word of God becomes an intrusion in the life of the believer, encountering him. In other words, the Word of God begins to spiritually transform the believer into the likeness of Christ. Discipleship is the catalyst for transformation.

THE TRINITARIAN GIFTS

God, the holy Trinity, has given the Church certain gifts to assist us in the discipleship process. These gifts enable its members to be empowered in following Christ. In Romans 12:6-8, the "grace" gifts are given to build up the Church. In 1 Corinthians 12:7-10, the Holy Spirit gives supernatural manifestations to each spirit-filled believer, "just as he determines" (v. 11). These manifestations are given to minister to the needs of all the believers. In Ephesians 4:7-11, Jesus the Christ gave gifts to men (the Church) as apostles, prophets, evangelists, pastors, and teachers. These ministry gifts were given to provide God's people for works of service and that they would no longer be infants (vv. 12-14).

A theology of discipleship must not ignore these particular gifts and manifestations. They are critical to spiritual growth, which promotes church growth. Their existence must be properly taught, tapped, and utilized for the benefit of the Church. In other words, the Church must make room for the Trinitarian gifts.

Accountability

A theology of discipleship must include accountability and disciplinary measures. The accountability must take place overall—upward and downward, from the pulpit to the pew. No one is exempt. In his letter to the church in Rome, Paul addresses this with the Jews, concerning the law:

> If you know his will and approve of what is superior because you are instructed by the law; if you are convinced that you are a guide for the blind, a light for those who are in the dark, an instructor of the foolish, a teacher of infants, because you have in the law the embodiment of knowledge and truth—you, then, who teach others, do not teach yourself? You who preach against stealing, do you steal? You who say that people should not commit adultery, do you commit adultery? You who abhor idols, do you rob temples? You who brag about the law, do you dishonor God by breaking the law? As it is written: "God's name is blasphemed among the Gentiles because of you." (Rom. 2:18-24).

Paul does not "bite his tongue" when it comes to accountability. We who are involved in discipleship training must "practice what we preach/teach." The disciple must be a reliable and responsible mentoring agent to those believers whom he is grooming in discipleship. New converts have left the church because of the blatant hypocrisy exhibited by the supposedly more mature Christians.

Paul thrashes the accountability whip downward in 1 Corinthians 5. The apostle reprimands the Corinthian church for its lack of disciplinary action concerning the sexual immorality of one of its members. Paul says to the church:

> And you are proud! Shouldn't you rather have been filled with grief and have put out of your fellowship the man who did this? . . .When you are assembled in the name of our Lord Jesus . . . and the power of our Lord Jesus is present, hand this man over to Satan, so that the sinful nature may be destroyed and his spirit saved on the day of the Lord. (1 Cor. 5:2-5)

Church accountability and discipline are sanctioned by the Word of God, and extends in every direction. A theology of discipleship embraces this.

CONCLUSION

Discipleship is not an easy feat. Jesus was very serious concerning His proclamation of discipleship: to deny one's self, take up one's cross, and follow Him. Thus, a theology of discipleship must proclaim the same demand. Discipleship is the key to real church growth.

A theology of discipleship commands Kingdom living from all of us who desire and profess to follow Christ. Those who are to make disciples are to forge ahead, in the name of Jesus Christ and in the power of the Holy Spirit, becoming the paradoxes of the world. Jesus gave the expectations in the Beatitudes. The result is that we become the salt of the earth, never to lose our savor (Matt. 5:13) and the light of the world, not to be hidden but to shine before men that they may *see* our good deeds and glorify our Father (Matt. 5:14, 16).

Discipleship commands a "tall act" to follow Jesus Christ. Paul puts it succinctly when he challenges the disciples to imitate Christ's humility, servitude, and obedience (Phil. 2:5-8). Before that proclamation of Jesus Christ, Paul calls us out as we proclaim to be followers of Christ:

> If you have any encouragement from being united with Christ, if any comfort from his love, if any fellowship with the Spirit, if any tenderness and compassion, then make my joy complete by being like-minded, having the same love, being one in spirit and purpose. Do not out of selfish ambition or vain conceit, but in humility consider others better than yourselves. Each of you should look not only at your own interests, but also to the interests of others. Your attitude should be the same as that of Christ Jesus. (Phil. 5:1-5)

This is the crux of a true theology of discipleship.

PART THREE

A STRATEGIC PLAN AND IMPLEMENTATION FOR CHURCH GROWTH

A strategic plan for church growth at Trinity United Christian Church (TUCC) must be developed on several levels. TUCC was entrenched in traditionalism and yet, it is fast approaching postmodernism. A methodology must, therefore, take into consideration both the traditional and postmodern components of this church, which will involve a tremendous amount of work and energy. In one worship service, there are four generations that share in the message of the Gospel of Jesus Christ. Although His message is eternal, each generation processes this message differently. As was previously iterated, we must not change the message of the Gospel, but we must change the method that we use to deliver and sustain it in the lives of humankind.

A strategic methodology for church growth must, emphatically, involve evangelism and discipleship. The full proclamation of the "good news," along with the initiation into the Kingdom of God and Christian maturation are conducive to real church growth. This methodology must not only rescue those who are lost (both in and out of the church) and nurture them for Kingdom living, but it must also train and equip disciples to make disciples. The process of fulfilling Jesus' mandate in the *Great Commission* culminates in disciples fulfilling acts of both evangelism and discipleship.

In this section, I discuss TUCC's strategic plan for church growth, the methodologies of evangelism and discipleship that would engage this plan, and the practical implementation of this strategic plan for church growth. In Chapter 6, I develop a strategic plan for church growth at TUCC. As previously mentioned, TUCC is experiencing an intrusion upon its traditional way of life. The generations that we must seek to present the Gospel to are those who make up the majority of our society—the postmodernists. This strategic plan must address both the traditionalists and the postmodernists of the TUCC congregation. With this in mind, the church's slogan, *Winning, Discipling, and Serving*, is the umbrella over this strategic plan. I as the pastor, emphasized and implemented the initial conduit of both evangelism and discipleship to enact this slogan. The development of an evangelistic mission statement for the church creates a focal point for the evangelism methodology. The mission statement is further defined by four core values: *worship*, *spiritual development*, *stewardship*, and *missions*. The strategic plan is the basis for spiritual growth at TUCC.

In Chapter 7, I will present a methodology for evangelism and a methodology for discipleship, in the context of TUCC. These methodologies stem from the church's strategic plan for church growth. Methodologies are contingent upon the cultural atmosphere of the church, as well as how the church perceives and plans for church growth. These methodologies evolve from the biblical foundations on which modern-day evangelism and discipleship are built. The theologies of evangelism and discipleship, as outlined in Chapter 5, play an integral part in the development of their respective methodologies.

In Chapter 8, I attend to the practical implementation of the strategic plan. This implementation centers around a small groups ministry that assimilates and cultivates new members into the whole of church life at TUCC. Small groups ministry focuses on empowering the laity for ministry that they may "go and make disciples."

To this task, let us turn!

CHAPTER SIX

A STRATEGIC PLAN FOR CHURCH GROWTH

Tools for effective church growth require a biblical foundation and a developed theology. Additionally, a methodology for church growth in a postmodern context is essential. This chapter begins our discovery of how we placed the pieces together in TUCC's context.

Leadership has become a major thrust at TUCC. Great potential exists when the pastor grows and implements his leadership skills in the congregation. C. Peter Wagner says that the vital sign of a growing church is a "pastor who is a possibility thinker and whose dynamic leadership has been used to catalyze the entire church into action for growth."[106] A church without an evangelistic minister will never reach out to the world. My responsibility was to guide the congregation toward an evangelistic outreach, as I was guided by the Holy Spirit. As their pastor, my purpose remained to initiate the passion and teaching for evangelism and discipleship that will shape and mold the people toward viable church growth.

106 C. Peter Wagner, *Your Church Can Grow*, 57.

In this chapter, it is essential to first address the conflicts and resolutions present when a traditional congregation becomes infiltrated by the postmodern world. The bottom line for today's churches, in this twenty-first century, is that we are now living in a postmodern era. Its constituents, the Generations X and Y, millennials (or whatever else we have labeled them) are in conflict with its baby-boomer and senior predecessors, their parents and grandparents (and maybe even great-grandparents).

The creation of an evangelistic mission statement helped guide this church in its church growth. This mission statement paints a very broad stroke to include discipleship. In this context, we are committed to "making disciples of all nations."

The essence of TUCC's mission is motivated by its core values, shrouded under the umbrella of its slogan, *Winning, Discipling, and Serving*. They are *worship*, *spiritual development*, *stewardship*, and *missions*, formed by the elders of this church. These values are the pillars that support the church's mission. If each one is strong, the church will move forward in its mission. *Worship* draws us into the presence of God. *Spiritual development*, through spiritual disciplines and Christian education, places our foot on a solid foundation. A theology of *stewardship* teaches everyone that all we have belongs to God. *Missions* covers the entire spectrum of evangelism and discipleship, implementing a "social" gospel as well. All four values effect our mission to the world. When any one pillar becomes weak, then our mission for Christ will be less than God established it to be.

Our goal is not a building or monument. Our objective is to reach people for Christ. We seek to achieve this through evangelism and discipleship, by developing a strategic plan for church growth.

TRADITIONAL VS. POSTMODERN

For the past one hundred years, TUCC has gone through many changes. However, in the past twenty-five years, change has been exponential. We now live in what has become a new and strange cultural context; we are experiencing a paradigm shift from the modern age to the postmodern age.

At TUCC, the blue-collar traditional church of the twentieth century was defined by doctrine, organs, books, and quaint buildings. Traditionalism worked. The culture embraced this style and many people came to know Jesus Christ as Lord and Savior. Dedicated individuals willingly sacrificed their time and fortunes to see God's will accomplished in people's lives. Sunday school and the King James Version of the Bible became normative in church life. As a nation, our culture, ideals, and values were shaped by the church. However, during the second half of the last century, the traditional lifestyles that characterized so many families began to crumble. After World War II, the family unit began its slow descent to disintegration. The '60s, '70s, and '80s saw a new world emerging, one that the traditional church has difficulty accepting and understanding.

Clearly, the postmodern culture has permeated our lives. Skepticism and suspicion are the inner values of our society, and absolute truth is denied at every level. We discovered that the culture of TUCC was foreign to a postmodernist's life and experience. The traditional model of church does not reach out to a postmodern world. The focus of TUCC was to take care of its own members and not reach the people outside of its building. The traditional church methods of TUCC did not fit into the cultural patterns of the postmodernists. Yet, postmodernism is a mixed blessing in that there are many opportunities for the Gospel. TUCC has come to realize that today's world is a postmodern world and that we engage this world in our schools, through television, and in the marketplace (where we work and do business). Why do we suddenly fall back into a 1950s mindset when we walk through our church doors? What will we, at TUCC, do to reach new people with the gospel message? Will this church blend the two ages (modernity and postmodernity) or become one way or the other? Our traditional church needs a fundamental shift from maintenance to mission.

TUCC began to take this postmodern culture seriously by trying to reach people from that culture. This concept stretched the church beyond its comfort zone. We started to think like missionaries. As a pastor of one church put it, "You do it like you do on the mission field . . . indigenous Christianity engages the population you want to reach. That means using the language they understand and adopting to their cultural styles in any way you can."[107] The traditionalists became outraged. They felt that their integrity and hard work were being threatened. "Traditional churches usually assume that cultural integrity requires them to perpetuate the cultural forms that God blessed in the past."[108] In the chaos, the postmodernists began to leave. They concluded that God was not interested in people like themselves. Eventually, through prayer and hard work, a new group of people emerged who understood both the traditional and postmodern worlds. We pushed the envelope in evangelism. We taught the people, through sermons and Bible studies, that a new world was in our midst. We would lose this world and generation if we did not realize Christ's command to go into this world and touch people in their own way.

Control in our traditional church empowered illegitimate accountability in the membership. Our postmodern approach

107 As quoted by George C. Hunter, III and Bruce Larson, *Church for the Unchurched* (Nashville: Abingdon, 1996), 155.

108 Ibid., 56.

releases trust. Today we have Bible Study groups that focus on the work and ministry of the Holy Spirit. Worship services centered on prayer and healing. The youth ministry is led by anointed leaders. This is imaginative as well as creative. For many, however, this is frightful. We have opened the boundaries of the church to include more people in ministry. Several changes have taken place. For instance: (1) the board has become less powerful and does not shape the identity of the congregation; (2) the annual meetings refine, define, and celebrate the goals of the church; and (3) the pastor is more than a puppet or governed CEO. Lay people are finding fulfillment in their positions. We have discovered that the Holy Spirit is guiding everyone, though our gifts are different (Rom. 12:6-8; 1 Cor. 12:7-10; Eph. 4:8-12). The mission of the church is to nurture people in the gifts God has given them. Trust is growing; distrust is vanishing.

WINNING, DISCIPLING, AND SERVING

This short, pithy, three-word slogan is the motto that TUCC has chosen to represent the mission of this church. Although this is a catchy phrase, it means absolutely nothing unless it is lived out specifically and tangibly in the life of the church. This motto is the umbrella of our strategic plan for church growth. It is the foundation from which the evangelistic mission statement and core values emerge.

WINNING

"He who wins souls is wise" (Prov. 11:30). At TUCC, our first and foremost objective is to develop a passion for winning souls to Christ. This is not a high sales pitch or manipulative ploy.

Winning souls involves TUCC living the *Great Commission* given to us by Jesus. Jesus said, "What good is it for a man to gain the whole world, and yet lose or forfeit his very self?" (Luke 9:25). Peter reminds us that Jesus is not in any big hurry to fulfill the promise of His second coming. It is more important that souls be saved. "The Lord is not slow in keeping his promise, as some understand slowness. He is patient with you, *not wanting anyone to perish, but everyone to come to repentance*" (2 Pet. 3:9, emphasis mine). Again, for this to be accomplished, we have been mandated to "make disciples of all nations."

DISCIPLING

Jesus told His disciples, "If anyone comes to me and does not hate his father and mother, his wife and children, his brothers and sisters—yes, even his own life—he cannot be my disciple. And anyone who does not carry his cross and follow me cannot be my disciple" (Luke 14:26-27). This is a critical statement and must be treated as such. When one follows Jesus, his life is no longer his own; his life now belongs to Jesus. He is truly a disciple of Christ.

It is discipleship that marks true church growth. To this we must commit a substantial effort. It is discipleship that leads to and comes out of evangelism. Jesus' three-year ministry was concentrated on making disciples for the Kingdom of God. The emphasis is on entering the Kingdom of God. It is our intention at TUCC to make disciples so that all who commit to be disciples will truly deny himself, take up his cross and truly follow Jesus Christ.

SERVING

The premier goal of discipleship is servanthood. Jesus was called the Suffering Servant, and we who are His followers must suffer in our service to others on behalf of Jesus. After Jesus was baptized, He stood up in the synagogue and read from the Isaiah scroll: "The Spirit of the Lord is on me, because he has anointed me to preach good news to the poor, He has sent me to proclaim freedom for the prisoners and recovery of sight for the blind, to release the oppressed, to proclaim the year of the Lord's favor" (Luke 4:18-19). This is the mark of a *servant*: to preach, teach, heal, and cast out demons, in the name of Jesus Christ.

True discipleship must be manifested in a life committed to service. This servanthood must reach far beyond the confines of our church building, to one's family, job, and the whole of society. Discipleship takes the hard road. Interaction with people and circumstances in this world is how Christ will touch a disciple's community. Service causes us to reach beyond our inner circle. Service is selfless discipleship, living out in human flesh the message of the cross. Our entire life becomes our worship and service to God. Jesus said:

> Then the King will say to those on his right, "Come, you who are blessed by my Father; take your inheritance, the kingdom prepared for you since the creation of the world. For I was hungry and you gave me something to eat, I was thirsty and you gave me something to drink, I was a stranger and you invited me in, I needed clothes and you clothed me, I was sick and you looked after me, I was in prison and you came to visit me. . . .I tell you the truth, whatever you did for one of the least of these brothers of mine, you did for me. (Matt. 25:34-40)

Winning, discipling, and serving: This clear and winsome slogan captures the essence of TUCC. The growth seen in the life of a disciple will be demonstrated in these three words. True transformation is the final objective of this strategy.

Developing an Evangelistic Mission Statement

The development of a clear understanding of the driving focus of the church is essential for the church that wishes to move forward. One may have a thoroughly developed church growth theology and not experience real church growth. Likewise, there can be a clearly articulated mission statement with no forward movement. In order for our church to accomplish its God-given task of making disciples of Jesus Christ, we must do both effectively. We must clearly articulate both effectively; theology and mission. In doing so, we must not fail to recognize that the church is both the living Body of Christ and a voluntary human organization.[109]

George Barna defines vision for Christian ministry more specifically as "a clear mental image of a preferable future, imparted by God, self, and circumstances."[110] A vision is the ability to see things that do not exist and bring them into being (Heb. 11:1). Vision is God's dream for us; it understands the past, present, and future. This clear articulation of theology and mission forms the church's vision. Every church should adopt the vision that they believe most clearly guides that church. "Where there is no vision, the people perish" (Prov. 29:18).

The specific vision for each individual congregation can, and should probably, be unique. However, that vision should embrace

109 Lyle Schaller, *Parish Planning: How to Get Things Done in the Church* (Nashville: Abingdon, 1971), 11.

110 George Barna, *Church Marketing: Breaking Ground for the Harvest* (Ventura, CA: Regal Books, 1992), 121.

an evangelistic endeavor of accomplishment. The vision reflects and defines the emphasis of the church's personality. Some churches do evangelism front door, side door, by friendship, and one-on-one. All churches, to accomplish the *Great Commission*, must do evangelism, but its vision of such reflects a God-given character. One of the common mistakes that we wish to avoid in developing a mission statement at TUCC is to uncritically adopt the vision of a highly successful church and assume that their mission and goals will work in our situation. Church growth writers warn against this potential pitfall. Each situation is unique and demands a unique application of the church growth principles.[111]

The first step in developing a strategic plan is for the pastor to acquire and state a vision. The vision must imagine the future of the church. It must be God's vision that the leader, members, and new members alike, can share in. My position at TUCC is to lead the people through a process of self-discovery. They must be challenged to reach a new generation of people. This process is important, thus, every person must participate.

The *Mission Statement* of TUCC was created by the elders and the board, both of which I am a part. It was a process that took several months in the making.

> *The purpose of this church is to make disciples of Jesus Christ in all the world, to teach them the exciting plans that the Lord has for their lives, and to commit them to actively work on behalf of the church.*

The key Scripture for this endeavor is: "*Therefore go and make disciples of all nations, baptizing them in the name of the Father and of the Son and of the Holy Spirit, and teaching*

111 Robert H. Craig and Robert C. Worley, *Dry Bones Live: Helping Congregations Discover New Life* (Louisville: John Knox, 1992), 17.

them to obey everything I have commanded you (Matt. 28:19, 20, emphasis mine).

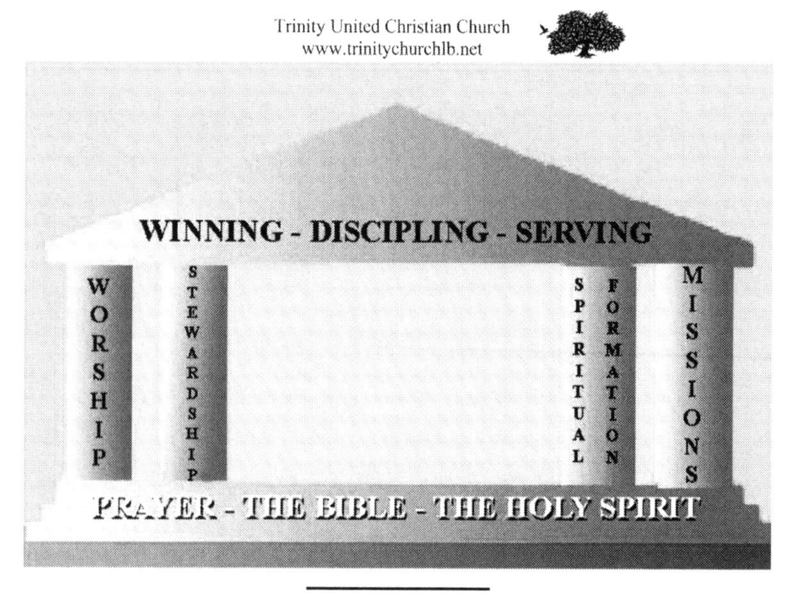

THE CORE VALUES

If a pastor desires to lead a congregation beyond a plateau and into growth, then he must communicate core values to the congregation. The leaders job is not to invent the future but rather discover the future to which God is calling His people. He must communicate it in a way that people will want to commit their lives to it.

Core values are the way things should be. They reflect the vision and mission of the church. The church's core values also reflect the culture of the church and are most easily disclosed in the statement "this is the way we do things around here." With a clear set of values and a philosophy of ministry in place, we do not have to react to emotions, personalities, or circumstances. We can be proactive and value-driven, because the values are clear.

The four core values of TUCC are: *worship*, *spiritual development*, *stewardship*, and *missions*. These values are central to the life of the church. They are convictions based on principles which direct our programs, sermons, and lay ministry. TUCC's clear philosophy of ministry has provided a clear sense of direction for the future of our church.

WORSHIP

Human beings are incurably religious. As we cannot live without air, our souls cannot live without worship. "Worshipping is as natural to us as breathing. We are drawn to worship as naturally as we are drawn to our next breath. Without worshipping, we do not fully live."[112] The daily life situations we face become meaningful as we worship and reach for God. The church meets fundamentally to worship God in the gathering of His people. Hence, "two of the most important things the church does are to worship the God and Father of our Lord Jesus Christ and to witness to God's mighty acts of creation, redemption and sanctification."[113] God Himself is the central attraction of the church.

Dean M. Kelly, of the National Council of Churches, challenged liberal Protestantism in his book *Why Conservative Churches are Growing*. He states that most liberal denominations have declined at an alarming rate because they neglect the central attraction of the church, God. He says we must "explain life in ultimate terms."[114] Churches which lose sight of the basic spiritual hungers of their people are destined to lose the very

112 Kennon Callahan, *Dynamic Worship* (San Francisco: Jossey-Bass, 1997), 3.

113 Frank Senn, *The Witness of the Worshipping Community* (New York: Paulist, 1993), 5.

114 Dean M. Kelly, *Why Conservative Churches are Growing* (San Francisco: Harper&Row, 1972), 37.

ones who are most likely to turn to God in the first place, people who are searching for the ultimate, God.

The major components of congregational worship are: "the service is warm and dynamic, the music is dynamic and inspiring, the service has power and movement, the services and sanctuary help the congregation reach persons in the community in mission, the preaching expresses the character of the Gospel and the quality of compassion."[115] However, all of this must be Christ-centered.

TUCC has been in the process of changing from a traditional church to a blended form that also embraces the postmodern individual. The leadership has recognized the need to reach a new generation. Therefore, the style of music has totally changed. People are encouraged to move, raise their hands and say "Amen." We are not trying to be Baptist or Pentecostal; we just want the congregation to be interactive and responsive. They are not to be spectators but willing participants in the worship of God. The denial of body motion and movements is a tragic subtraction from the whole of one's praise. We want people to connect with God.

Our praise team, Crossbound, leads our contemporary worship in praise and joyful worship every Sunday.

115 Callahan, *Dynamic Worship*, 5.

In addition, the worship of God is not a psychological experience filled with happy moments. TUCC desires that people be challenged and uplifted at the same time. If the worship is only about good feelings, then we have missed the point. "We will not have met God. A true encounter with God leaves us with a lot more than good feelings. It leaves us with changed hearts and calls us to changed lives. Very simply, to experience God's presence is to be transformed from the inside out."[116] Our goal in worship is to have a roomful of worshipers who are so filled with God's presence that it saturates the families and friendships they have beyond the four walls of the church. Hence, their entire lives become their worship to God.

I believe worship can be the greatest evangelism vehicle we have. When someone is sitting with a group of authentic people who are looking at the screen and singing music in their style, it touches the heart. Simple declarations about the awesomeness of God can create an aura that fills the room. The transcendence and immanence of God are revealed in such a setting. It moves postmodern individuals to see the sincere worship of something totally other. Their world is so fractured, that a glimpse into the heart of God melts the hardness that has been built. When they experience God invading their space, it engages that inner part of their spirit that has been dormant for so long. Jack Hayford, pastor of The Church on the Way in Van Nuys, California, offers these thoughts:

> I am totally persuaded that worship is the key to evangelism as well as to the edification of the Church. . . . As worship moves beyond a merely objective exercise demanded by theological posturing, and as it becomes a simple, subjective quest for God, He responds. . . . I contend that, as long as worship is focused on

116 Sally Morgenthaler, *Worship Evangelism: Inviting Unbelievers into the Presence of God* (Grand Rapids: Zondervan, 1999), 52.

> protecting God from unworthy participants, it can never serve His purpose as a resource for incomplete and broken mankind to find completion and wholeness in His presence.[117]

God is seeking worshipers who will lead others to Christ. Their worship of God will trigger the inner desire to seek God. TUCC's purpose for worship starts with this premise in mind.

At TUCC, the people are included in the planning of a worship service. Their characters, personalities, needs, struggles, hopes, and dreams become a part of the worship experience. Prayer and sharing go into the plan. We welcome suggestions to make the worship service user-friendly to postmodernists and pre-Christians. The wisdom of the people is essential to the process. The word *liturgy* means "the work of the people." Why not allow their input into the celebration?

Finally, worship was never intended to be a passive event. It requires action, both by the people and the pastor. Worship spotlights the Trinity: Father, Son, and Holy Spirit. Worship is not a seminar or lecture presentation or a promotional situation. We worship because within all of us is a craving to reach toward the transcendent. Are we willing to open our worship celebrations to postmodernists and reach a new generation?

SPIRITUAL DEVELOPMENT

This core value has more to do with being than doing. A vital congregation must know who they are and not become just an outlet of productivity. Two areas will be discussed here: Christian education and spiritual disciplines. The teaching

117 Jack Hayford, *Worship His Majesty: How Praising the King of Kings Will Change Your Life* (Waco, TX: Word Books, 1987; Ventura, CA: Regal Books, 2000).

and training which will happen at TUCC is essential to the growth of the church.

Our continued growth at TUCC will depend on the quality of Christian education we can give. Christian education must be more then listening to lectures and receiving information. Postmodernists are not conducive to sitting and listening to lectures, most of which they do not understand, nor can they relate them. Their world is participatory and interactive. Just look at the music videos, Youtube videos, and the time that they spend on the Internet. They must be able to relate their real-life experiences to the experiences of and in the Bible. Christian educators must be able to take the biblical stories and passages and relate them in such a way as to formulate life applications for individual and collective accountability. This is critical, so that they may embrace the Word of God, come to know and understand a true and living God, and thus begin to build a loving and lasting relationship with God. This is essential before the church can prepare them to reach outside of their own boundaries into a world which they understand and can help to make a difference in the lives of others. Field education opportunities (missions trips at home and abroad) will open the minds of the postmodernists, bringing them out of their individualism, to care about and care for others.

Essentially, the goal in Christian education is transformation through discipleship. First, the individuals must be brought into a transformative environment and then they are to be discipled in order that they may eventually evangelize and make disciples. Lawrence Richards defines Christian education in a very succinct way: "Christian education is different. In Christian education, our focus is on life. In Christian education, our goal is transformation. In Christian education, the total community is involved. In Christian education, modeling and interpersonal relationships are critical concerns."[118]

A dynamic Christian education program will be a discipleship strategy which helps the disciple grow in the character and image of Jesus Christ. Likewise, the entire community will be involved. Parents and children must grow together in faith. In a society that divides people into groups, intergenerational teaching is a must in order that we may close the generation gap that exists within the church. The church is one of the few places left in our culture where various generations are asked to relate to each others' needs and concerns.

With four generations of people in our church setting, the range and diversity of Christian education must be flexible. A structured mainline approach will stifle a new disciple. However, a creative Christian education program which understands the culture of the postmodern world and is willing to relate the Gospel to it, will be much more effective. TUCC must break out of the traditional molds of "Sunday only" and lecture-style teaching. Our methods of teaching Christian education must be relevant and up-to-date. A Christian education that will allow for open-ended questions will be attractive to a postmodern mind. True Christian education will not take the power of the Spirit and institutionalize it.

Discipleship means there is discipline involved; both terms evolve from the same root. A forgotten practice among many Christians are the spiritual disciplines. These are time honored, Scripture-based methods to focus our being on God and His presence. The spiritual disciplines are a lost art in the church. TUCC must turn to those practices which Christians for centuries have lived in their normal Christian

118 Lawrence O. Richards, *A Theology of Christian Education*, 47.

lives. A postmodern sojourner may appreciate the mystery and experiential nature of these practices. They are more spiritually based, which is what most postmodernists are searching for today, a greater depth of spirituality.

At TUCC, fasting has been encouraged with the congregation. Individuals have taken upon themselves to fast for specific situations and people. We felt a connectedness that was not known in our prayers and worship. Likewise, fasting has been uplifted for the Lenten and Easter seasons of the church year. Many members are from orthodox and catholic backgrounds and their spiritual upbringing involved these practices. TUCC will continue to promote fasting, with our prayer ministry, because fasting has changed many lives. However, we will have to rethink how we will encourage and assist the postmodern generations in fasting. In a world in which we are obsessed with eating, where fast-food restaurants are on every corner and television advertisements promote quick-fix foods, we must institute various kinds of fasting, after having taught on the purpose and effectiveness of fasting. Fasting is a serious discipline and must be treated as such.

In a postmodern world, there is a hunger for spiritual encounters. Intentional and structured prayer time is provided every Sunday morning. There is silence, a time for sharing of concerns and open prayer time. Likewise, if someone has a "word from the Lord" they are encouraged to share this word. The person who leads this "word" has a background in charismatic renewal. His orientation to the Holy Spirit's presence brings a perfect blend of the moving of the Spirit with the structure. He is gentle but firm with what occurs. This encounter has had only adult participation but a future style for the postmodern youth is being studied.

We know that prayer time must be more interactive with the youth, yet several of them yearn for moments of silence and quiet. One form of prayer that would be quite effective for postmodernist to engage in is called *Lectio Divina*. This prayer form is conducted wherein a facilitator reads a very small passage of Scripture (as certainly led by the Holy Spirit). The participants quietly meditate as they hear the Scripture being read, and afterwards. The purpose is to open one's heart to hear God speaking to him through the Scripture being read. The facilitator then asks a question for the hearers to meditate on and seek God's presence. The Scripture passage is read three more times, with meditation, question, and discussion intervals. This is done in a small group setting, so that group members can share what they "hear" and pray for each other at the end of this session. Spiritual disciplines are meant to be experienced.

Spiritual development is a process that we at TUCC are still learning. The Roman Catholic background of many of our parishioners helps us to envision great possibilities for acceptance and growth in this area. (Roman Catholic teachings have their emphasis in spiritual disciplines.) The more we can apply spiritual development to TUCC, the more discipleship will take place, and God's church can grow.

STEWARDSHIP

What God made good, we have succeeded in misusing. Biblical stewardship was never the image of offering plates filled with money (the image most church-goers have of stewardship). Rather, it was designed to be an exhaustive reference to all there is in our lives. It is the sum total of one's life, wealth, and gifts given as a response of faith.

God's Word directs us to see all of our life as a gift to God and people. The Apostle Paul writes, "Therefore, I urge you, brothers, in view of God's mercy, to offer your bodies as living sacrifices, holy and pleasing to God—this is your spiritual act of worship" (Rom. 12:1). Luke, Paul's counterpart on his missionary journeys, records, "all the believers were together and had everything in common. Selling their possessions and goods, they gave to anyone as he had need" (Acts 2:44-45). It is clear that one's possessions and wealth, along with the contributions to the ministry, were the trademarks of Christian stewardship. Hence, stewardship is an act of worship.

For many church members, stewardship is money. This is not biblical. All our behavior and life belongs to God and must be freely given. "Stewardship relates . . . to how and in what ways we use everything God has given us. It includes our use of this created world and the space around it, life itself, our time, our skills, our relationships to people and things."[119] Therefore, although our money is involved, it is not the focus. We must be obedient stewards with our entire lives. When stewardship is taught from this perspective, the money will come.

Jesus speaks continually about the use of our possessions. He was not only concerned with the life beyond this one. He knew that we had to live in this world and His incarnation as a human being shows us the way. In several of His parables our Lord tells us of the temptations of riches (Luke 12:15-21) and the eternal consequences of the misuse of possessions (Luke 16:19-31). In fact, "it is established that fully one-sixth of all the words of Jesus in the New Testament are concerned with this one subject, and over one-third of all Jesus' parables are devoted to it. The fact is that the subject Jesus talked about more than any other was the

119 John H. MacNaughton, *Stewardship: Myths and Methods—A Program Guide for Ministers and Lay Leaders* (New York: Seabury, 1975), ix.

proper use of one's possessions."[120] Jesus understood better than anyone that our material surroundings could control our lives. A proper theology of stewardship in a church is needed for that church to grow and thrive.

A theology of stewardship begins with God in creation. God gave all of humankind stewardship over the earth (Gen. 1:28-30). Throughout the Old Testament, the Lord reminds His people that everything comes from His hand (Deut. 8:18; Hag. 2:8). Therefore, He asks that we give a portion of our material life to His work (Gen. 14:20; Deut. 14:22). This "tithe" is to pay for the upkeep of the church and to give to the poor of the community. That is why God is disgusted when we hold back our giving for selfish motives. In fact, He calls it stealing (Mal. 3:8-9). We have misused God's resources and it creates problems in our lives, families, and churches. A theology of stewardship must emphasize the spiritual responsibility we have toward God and each other.

In the New Testament, Jesus asks us to give Him all of our lives, including our possessions. Our commitment to discipleship includes an inventory of all that we have and own. In the parable of the rich man, Jesus invites a person to give up everything to follow Him. However, the rich man cannot do this because he loves his riches too much (Mark 10:17-22). Earlier in the same Gospel, Jesus challenges the people, saying, "What good is it for a man to gain the whole world, yet forfeit his soul?" (Mark 8:36). In the Gospels, essentially what Jesus is asking us, "Who or what are you really worshipping?" Our stewardship must convey the idea that our entire lives belong to God. We do not have anything God has not given us. We did not earn anything. Hence, in the end, when we give all to

120 Ibid., 7.

Jesus in discipleship He will reward us with a fulfilling life and eternal rewards (Mark 10:28-30).

Postmodern people are looking for more than what this material world gives. They desire a life that fulfills the spiritual longing in their spirit. A biblical theology of stewardship will awaken their being. They will respond with joy and enthusiasm when they realize that material life is secondary. A life truly lived for Christ and others is the only life that gratifies.

MISSIONS

At this point in human history, the population of the world is approximately eight billion people. One third of the world is Christian. Another third calls themselves Muslim. The need is great for men and women of God to go reach the lost for Christ.

The Bible itself is a book about missions. Throughout its pages, both in the Old and New Testaments, ideas of missions and world evangelism stand out. In the Old Testament, the lives of Abraham, Joseph, and Elijah carried God's message to other parts of the world. In the life of Moses we see the life of mission. Other prophets, such as Jonah, Jeremiah, and Amos, had the missionary spirit.

In the New Testament, the call for missions is even greater. Simeon proclaimed Jesus Christ as "a light for revelation to the Gentiles and for glory to your people Israel" (Luke 2:32). Christ traveled throughout ancient Palestine with His message from the Father. After the Gospels, the book of Acts is a complete story dealing with a missionary church. The life of the Apostle Paul shows great missionary zeal. There can be no doubt that evangelism and missions are central to the teaching of the Bible.

We are called to reproduce disciples. The *Great Commission* is an invitation to the local church to touch this world for God. When Christ said, "I will build my church" (Matt. 16:18), it was a great declaration. With the "good news" of Christ in our hearts, we are commanded to penetrate new regions to communicate God's Word and create His community.

If the key to missions rests with the local church, then the focal point must rest on the pastor. It must be up to the pastor to preach and promote missions from the pulpit. The church can set up and support missionaries as they pray to see the world come to Christ. The pastor must have a local home missions emphasis. If the pastor is not concerned about the people next door, how can he be concerned with people in the next state, country, and/or continent. If the people do not see a missions emphasis in the pastor, how will they feel the need to be a missionary church, both at home and abroad. Thus, a pastor's own position on winning the lost is extremely important to the missionary outreach of the church.

Dean Gartland, CEO of Washington City Mission spoke of our support of homeless people in Washington PA, on our Missions Sunday

On our annual Missions Sunday, we spotlight, share and support the numerous missions that make Trinity a missions-minded church. Here is a list of just a few of the missions our Trinity members bolsters with their financial gifts:

- AVAC-Allegheny Valley Association of Churches, Natrona Heights PA
- Christian Church in PA-Camp Laurelview
- Family Fun Nights at Trinity
- Grace Food Pantry at Trinity
- Prayer Quilt Ministry at Trinity
- Tri-Life Center Baby Bottle Campaign. Lower Burrell PA
- Operation Christmas Child
- Pittsburgh Homeless Ministry-Lunches, Hot Dinners
- Souper Bowl of Caring
- Urban Impact-Pittsburgh, Northside, Pittsburgh PA
- Washington City Mission, Washington PA
- Womens' Ministry-Freezer Meals

Missions need not necessarily be overseas. Many times when "missions" is mentioned the average person's mind immediately begins to think of a place far away from home. Yet, those people are not the only ones in need of Christ's redeeming grace. There are many towns and communities in need of the gospel message. There are rescue and homeless missions which touch the lives of people less fortunate. Thus, the work of missions can be carried out on the home front as well.

At TUCC, we are still building a missions emphasis. We have become a "launching pad" for mission trips to New Kensington, Puerto Rico, Myrtle Beach, and Nicaragua with our youth ministry. The adults, as well, have traveled on short-term mission trips to Mexico, Sabine Pass (Texas), and Africa. Our church supports three local mission outreaches.

The first is a monthly homeless missions emphasis, wherein several members of the church have taken upon themselves, in cooperation with other churches, to go into downtown Pittsburgh to feed homeless men, women, and children. They believe in Jesus words, "whatever you did for one of the least of these brothers of mine, you did for me" (Matt. 25:40). Youth and adults have participated. Each week meals are prepared and taken to people in the city. Witnessing and singing are a part of the evening. It has become a monthly event which has opened the eyes of the congregation to the world. Second, a missions outreach to children is presented every weekend in our junior church during Sunday worship. Through recreation, prayer, and music, children are ministered to in the Lower Burrell and Kiski valley area. And third, we participate with Allegheny Valley Association of Churches, Interfaith Hospitality Network (IHN). IHN provides shelter, meals and assistance for homeless families and alleviates homelessness by providing support and advocacy. Every few months, our church building houses, for a week, families who are displaced while they find a place to live. These three local missions are a part of our missions emphasis.

Our 1997 "Operation Puerto Rico" Mission Trip with our Trinity Youth and the Christian Church (Disciples of Christ). Our missions-minded emphasis includes local and world missions. That's my mother, Norma, waving in the back row!

Initially, we have gone where we believed God was working. Today, we are taking a strategic and planned direction. Focused prayer and study is being implemented in TUCC's missions ministry. For too long, TUCC has thought of its own church body as its only mission. Missions was done by someone else far away. In our postmodern, unchurched culture, we have discovered we need to be missionaries, too. In the future, the missions emphasis will network through Lower Burrell, Pennsylvania and around the world. Our missions will involve sacrifice and commitment. A servant's heart will motivate our missions thrust. The word's of Jesus, "unless a grain of wheat falls into the earth and dies, it remains alone . . . but if it dies it bears much fruit" (John 12:24), captures our missions spirit. Missions is a way of life, not a luxury or hobby.

As twenty-first century missionaries, we must become humble people who care for the lost world around them. At TUCC, we are working on this attitude. Living in America is not conducive to risking our lives in faith. We have it too comfortable. Our core value of missions will pull the congregation out of its comfort zone into a world that is starving for the saving message of Jesus Christ.

CHAPTER SEVEN

A PLAN FOR CHURCH GROWTH

A methodology is a plan of enacting a concept into a reality. A methodology for church growth seeks to investigate and accept specific methods that will catalyze church growth. These methods must be conducive to the specific congregation one seeks to "grow." Since church growth is contingent upon two biblical principles, evangelism and discipleship, then its methodology should be contingent upon the effective methods through which evangelism and discipleship evolve.

In this chapter, I will discuss the methodologies of evangelism and discipleship in a postmodern context that specifically addresses the culture of TUCC as well as the culture of its surrounding community. These methodologies build on the core values of TUCC (as discussed in Chapter 6) as they relate to "winning, discipling, and serving."

Historically, the church universal has interpreted biblical evangelism through the lens of reason, tradition, and Scripture. The three legs of this *stool* help us to understand God. In today's postmodern world, another leg has been placed on the *stool*, called "my experience." Each person's experience is equal to another's; it is the American way. It is likened to a sign I noticed in a psychiatric hospital that said, "Reality is all in your imagination!" Whatever you want to believe is fine because it belongs to you. They measure life by their own self-appointed standards, not a transcendent one. However, there is one transcendent principle, proclaimed by Jesus Himself: that the Kingdom of God is near; repent and turn to Christ, for there is no other way. The need for truth and transcendence will always be greater than any cultural paradigm. Evangelism and discipleship in a postmodern era provide a uniquely fascinating challenge for TUCC. The methods we employ to the postmodernists will be strikingly different than those employed to a traditionalist. Let us proclaim the truth of Christ through the lens of this generation.

A Methodology of Evangelism in a Postmodern Context

One can easily see that a Christian worldview conflicts with much of what postmodernity teaches. Christianity claims to be true for everyone, everywhere. At TUCC, how do we as Christians evangelize a world that is diametrically opposed to Christ? How do we respond evangelistically? What issues in postmodernism can be redeemed to reach people for Christ? Our method of choice was not new. The adaptation of new music became the primary choice of change in methodology at TUCC.

Postmodernism is a combination of romantic optimism, that humankind can solve its social and economic problems, and a pessimism of never knowing absolute truth. It is an existentialist view of life searching for meaning in this life.

People are informed that they must confront an illogical existence with imposed meaning from the traditional church. This methodology of evangelism did not work. TUCC realized that we must do as the gospel evangelists did: present the Gospel from different perspectives. If the audience is hip-hop, rap, or metal-music oriented, the message of the Kingdom of God must be presented in those respective contexts. If youth are to be reached, our self-imposed rules must not be cast upon them.

Modeling after Jesus' method of evangelism, as discussed in Chapter 3, TUCC believes that we must begin with a methodology of incarnational evangelism—meeting people where they are, dwelling among them. Jesus never changed His message. The messages of the Kingdom, love, and forgiveness were always the same. However, He delivered these messages in different ways, utilizing the environment and lifestyles of the people. The context for Jesus' ministry went beyond the walls of the synagogue, although He also evangelized in the synagogues. He went to the people and touched them at the point of their needs. The way to evangelize a postmodern world is similar. Much of postmodernism gives a negative response to the confidence of modernism. TUCC had a set pattern to express its faith. Yet, we ignored the fact that our church was empty and our evangelism touched relatively no one.

THE HISTORICAL EVOLUTION OF EVANGELISM METHODOLOGY

In 1985, a task force comprised of various members of the congregation began to search for a creative way to reach people in New Kensington. After much study, debate, and prayer, a contemporary worship service was added, as a Saturday night service, in July 1997. Music was the major change. Though very few of the Sunday morning worshippers attended the Saturday night services, many curious people came to the church, drawn in by the music. People came off the streets to see what was happening. This was no ordinary church music: organ, piano, hymns. This music came from drums, guitars, and a keyboard. Weekend after weekend, we began to see a change. The Saturday night worship services were not without preaching and the sacrament of holy communion. However, the preacher was not adorned in an ecclesiastical garment and communion was conducted by the laity (not the elders). This evangelism methodology worked. The music was rendered by praise and worship choruses; the atmosphere was casual. People within the ages of thirty to forty-five dominated the services.

Saturday night was an excellent time for this community. For years, the Roman Catholic Church conducted Saturday evening masses. TUCC offered a Protestant form of worship that no other church held. We introduced a healing prayer session. Bible studies were held after the services, to introduce people to the Lord and His Word. We were unique (in the late 1990s) as we implemented these methods of evangelism to our context.

When TUCC moved to Lower Burrell in April 2000, the Saturday night music displaced the Sunday morning music. The leadership decided not to put a new organ in the building because they believed organ music was inappropriate for the twenty-first century. They figured that with such a major change as a church move, they could also revamp the music to attract a postmodern generation. Incrementally, the music was strategically changed to fit the Sunday morning worship experience. The keyboard, guitars, drums, and praise team of Saturday night became the music ministry of Sunday morning, the music of such groups as Integrity, Maranatha, Hosanna, Vineyard, and Hillsong. But only the music changed. The rest of the traditional morning worship service stayed the same. We kept the liturgical forms: the Lord's Prayer, the Doxology, the pastoral prayer, the words of institution, and the benediction.

We tried to blend the service to appeal to several generations within the congregation. However, this caused an upheaval in the church because the senior members were not familiar with the song lyrics. They asked, "Where are the old hymns?" Also, the loud drums and guitars adversely impacted their hearing. Several people wrote letters of complaint to the pastor. However, the appearance of the congregation also began to change. Many younger couples came to the church. Lower Burrell's community was younger and acceptance of the new music was immediate. To appease the senior members, the church added a traditional service, once a month, that would reinstate the hymns. However, only ten to fifteen people ever attended this service.

Between April 2000 and 2002, people were beginning to see that the traditional church was outdated. Many senior members either changed churches or did not come again. They were grieving over the loss of their church culture. Others saw the success and embraced the change. TUCC would never be the same, but it would not be enough.

The postmodernist's mind offers a unique challenge to TUCC. The children and youth are growing up in a postmodern environment. The Sunday morning worship service was still an outdated form of worship for them. To these youth, the contemporary praise music was slow compared to their fast-moving R&B, ska[121]/punk[122], and hip-hop music. Some of

121 A form of dance music, popular in Jamaica in the 1960s, characterized by the use of saxophones and other brass, a heavily accented offbeat, and the influence of New Orleans rhythm and blues, jazz, and calypso. http://www.dafunky-phish.com/HistoryofSka/.

122 Merriam Webster Online Dictionary, "Rock music marked by extreme and often deliberately offensive expression of alienation and social discontent," (Springfield, MA: Merriam Webster, Inc., 2002), http://www.m-w.com/cgi-bin/dictionary.

the rituals did not make sense to them. Questions such as, "Why do we repeat prayers that no one is thinking about?" were asked. In their world—school, home, and television—they have become accustomed to change and visual thought processes. They wanted more and expressed that desire vocally. They wanted to express their faith in a way that made sense to them and would bring them and their friends closer to Christ.

The debate over the music became messy and even combative at times. Their generation has been taught to be as bold and strong about their opinions as the older generations. The traditionalist at TUCC, on the one hand, fought to retain their styles of worship while the emerging postmodernists, on the other hand, sought to create something new.

The question before us today is very simple. Should we seek to appeal and accommodate this postmodern culture? At least one third, if not more, of our community is postmodern. If this is the path we choose to take, we have some major adjustments to make. We must work very hard at changing our image. In the eyes of a postmodernists, a traditional church looks like a irrelevant assembly. Of course, we can change our image without changing the essential message of the Gospel. We can become culturally relevant without compromising our beliefs. This will require a great deal of wisdom and courage. Our methodology will reflect our willingness to reach new people for our Lord.

The Adam's Rib youth band led the R.O.C.K. Night services with energetic music and worship for many young people in the Kiski Valley.

In February 2002, TUCC's youth ministry took a quantum leap of faith. They created a youth-led and inspired worship service, held once a month on Saturday nights. We called it R.O.C.K Night: Righteous Outpouring of Christ on Kids. Again, the music was the major difference, with a newly developed ska/punk band that played songs from Christian bands as well as those written by themselves. This band led the Saturday night worship services with their music. Other bands and singers eventually became involved. There was also drama and special lighting.

Teenagers preached the Gospel message and led the communion service. Attendance averaged over one hundred. Teenagers brought their friends, dawning red hair, leather jackets, body piercing, and chains. Most of these young people would never have stepped foot into a church, let alone a traditional church service. Our youth became the "evangelists," and many people came to accept Christ. The teenagers brought their issues and problems. There were messages on overcoming sexual immorality, drugs, and anger by faith in Jesus Christ. The medium of communication was nothing like Sunday morning. This postmodern generation was allowed to express itself the way they wanted. It was a genuine and authentic evening for teenagers to experience God. Other churches began to come see what was happening. For the first time, we met the parents of some of the youth. We were truly being missionaries to this postmodern community. The church was shocked, but they too have given their blessings to this form of worship. Postmodern youth were finding a home in our church.

An area in great need with the postmodern youth service is strong discipleship training. Though the music became the draw of the R.O.C.K. service, we noticed that this was only touching the surface of their spiritual lives. These postmodernists need to be grounded in the Word and prayer. The youth speakers require more personal training and mentoring. Even those who sing and lead the communion service need to know the importance of their actions before the worshipping congregation. We have trained several student leaders in evangelism and personal quiet time. However, much more emphasis must be given to the entire youth group so that the worship service is more than a social time together.

In essence, our youth and young adults are starving for spiritual encounters. Evangelism in a postmodern context breaks through the outward appearance, entering the core of a person's existence. Postmodernists have no need for self-appointed authority, yet there is an inner need for the transcendent. The postmodern evangelist is married to the message but not the method. He must be "wise as a serpent and gentle as a dove" (Matt. 10:16). There is a vast difference between ultimate truth and preferences. Evangelism is missionary work in a postmodern world. Just as we would send missiologists to a country or culture to evaluate the setting, so our evangelism must take the same energy and creativity. As our evangelism is contextualized to our situation, the Gospel can be 'incarnated' into peoples' lives. We can then begin to create the new methodologies we need for twenty-first century evangelism at TUCC.

KISKI VALLEY TODAY • JUNE 2002

Giving Youth A Place To Express Their Faith

Pastor Cletus Hull wasn't expecting the explosive growth that took place within the Trinity United Christian Church youth worship service. Since the inception of R.O.C.K. (Righteous Outpouring of Christ on Kids) a couple of months ago they've had over one

Pastor Cletus Hall

hundred in attendance at each monthly service. The last worship service that they had drew in 189 individuals. The night ended with eighteen of them being baptized. This is pretty impressive considering that the growth of this group has been entirely by word of mouth. The youth of the church receive tickets to hand out to their friends as invitations. These are brought back with them to be used for drawings for free pizza tickets, Christian CDs and "Adam's Rib" T-shirts.

When Pastor Hull decided to move forward with the youth worship service, he said that he would do it as long as there were no restrictions on the music or how the youth presented their portion of the night. "Who better to reach the youth in the community than other youth," stated Hull. And, it has grown beyond all their expectations.

"The music is the biggest draw for the teenagers, they love it," stated Pastor Hull. Their band "Adam's Rib" plays ska/punk/swing music. The

Trinity United Christian Church

band members are Ben & James Crytzer, Bryan Altman, and JJ Lavelle. They perform songs from other artists and also some of the songs that they have written. This summer they will be going to Myrtle Beach to play at campgrounds. They have already been able to raise enough money for the trip. The program that they are involved in is an Intercostals Outreach that deals with youth ministry in Myrtle Beach.

Besides the band, they perform drama, give a message, sing worship songs and have a time of fellowship at the end of the night. For the message they take turns with the girls and boys. They also have outside speakers. "The whole idea behind the youth group," Pastor Hull explained, "is to give the youth a place to worship God, express their faith in a way they can relate and understand best and provide a safe place to invite friends."

PROPOSED METHODOLOGIES FOR EVANGELISM

Music is not the only way to reach our postmodern generation. Not all of this generation will voluntarily set foot in anybody's church. Many in this generation never heard of God and come from atheistic families. Not all are into the music style exhibited in our Saturday night worship service. There are many effective methods in which we can reach out to this generation. Our hope at TUCC is to network with other churches who are reaching out to this postmodern generation and share techniques and methods for evangelism. The following methodologies for evangelism are just a few of what TUCC is considering in order to reach a postmodern generation.

PERSONAL EVANGELISM

Every believer should be engaged in personal evangelism, and is therefore an "evangelist" as an obligation, not a call.[123] However, it is imperative that those who communicate the message of the Gospel have a credible understanding of what that Gospel is and how to communicate it. It is also critical that the person who is evangelizing is one who believes and walks according to the Gospel. "In order for personal evangelism to have validity, particularly in these times, there must be coherence between the message and the messenger. The character of the person articulating the claims of the Gospel needs to coincide with the theory being communicated."[124]

There are many opportunities for each of us to share the Gospel of Jesus Christ: at home, school, nursing homes, where we work, prisons, apartment complexes, and on the bus/train/

123 "Evangelist" is used in quotations to distinguish the believer as doing evangelism from the evangelist that Jesus calls as part of the fivefold ministry (Eph. 4:11).

124 Posterski, *Reinventing Evangelism*, 125

subway/airplane/cruise ship. The Holy Spirit has a way of presenting opportunities for us to properly evangelize in a personal and personable way. There is no "set'" way to approach anyone; no predisposed formula. "Jesus was not an advocate of 'xerox evangelism.' Without compromising the truth of the message, he adapted his communication so that it applied to the circumstances of the person in his presence."[125]

Personal evangelism is not about coaxing someone to come and visit our church. For a postmodernist, that is a turn-off. The person whom you approach may be a hard-nosed skeptic who asks the hard questions, with lots of cynicism. Striking up a conversation with this person may lead to a further opportunity to share the Gospel, if only a glimpse. However, when doing personal evangelism, one must be very sensitive to the other person. Our attitude must be of genuine concern for the other person, even with the challenge of getting that person to hear us. "There is nothing in the New Testament record to indicate that Jesus ever conveyed an attitude toward people that called them to conform to his preferences before they received a serious hearing."[126] The "evangelist" must find out where that person's head and heart is before jumping headlong into a conversation about Jesus that might very well be just a lecture, as well as a turn-off.

In personal evangelism, proper dialogue is key. The "evangelist" must not only ask questions but allow the audience to equally ask questions. Personal evangelism occurs on any level and there is no need to feel pressured into deliberating the *full* gospel during one encounter. The Holy Spirit always has another "evangelist" to pick up where one "evangelist" left off, or He may give the same "evangelist" another opportunity to encounter this same person.

125 Ibid., 123.

126 Ibid., 117.

PRAYER EVANGELISM

This method of evangelism does not consider the full scope of evangelism. It is usually done in conjunction with another method of evangelism. Prayer evangelism is group prayer solely dedicated to the conviction of souls that have received the Gospel via other methods of evangelism. Jesus said, "Again, I tell you that if two of you on earth agree about anything you ask for, it will be done for you by my Father in heaven. For where two or three come together in my name, there I am with them" (Matt. 18:19-20). The prayer evangelism group need not be large; Jesus only requires two or three. This way many prayer evangelism groups can be formed to concentrate on one to three persons who have heard the Gospel, for their conviction and conversion.

SILENT EVANGELISM

How can the proclamation of the Gospel be a silent matter? Well, it cannot. However, in this postmodern era, we often have a hard time getting an audience to give us their ear and undivided attention. One method of doing this is to appeal to them from a relationship perspective, with no overt agenda. We can turn our fellowship hall into a coffee house and game room on Friday evenings for the sixteen to twenty-year olds. A place and time for us to just "hang out" with them, getting to know them and letting them get to know us. Within this context, there can be a one-on-one engagement of personal evangelism at the appointed, Spirit-led time. Or we can get really creative and lease a school gym, with no evidence of "church" to turn the youth off from hearing the Gospel. Again, only engaging in actual personal evangelism at the "appointed time."

In essence, like prayer evangelism, silent evangelism cannot be engaged as an isolated method. The proclamation goes forth *after* the "evangelist" has gained the trust of the postmodern youth.

SMALL GROUP EVANGELISM

This method of evangelism is for those actually seeking to know the Christ of the Church. This form of evangelism is a small group Bible study that presents Jesus—who He is and why He came to save us—His Gospel, and His death and resurrection. It is in this context of evangelism that new converts are initiated into the Kingdom of God that Jesus so clearly proclaimed as the requirement for becoming His disciple. Because of their rebellion against the establishment authority, it is critical that Jesus be presented as Lord as well as Savior, in the context of the Kingdom of God. They must come to understand that God's authority and power "holds water" and is the antithesis of worldly authority and power. They must come to understand that not only is God full of unconditional love, compassion, and infinite wisdom and understanding, but that He is also a jealous and angry God, full of wrath. All aspects of knowing God must be presented in an articulate and delicate manner, through the study of His Word.

The message of reconciliation is key here, because so many of our young come with all sorts of problems and issues for which they are feeling guilty and heavily burdened. It is also in this context of evangelism that these participants learn to take responsibility for evangelizing to their friends.

Small group evangelism can take place within the confines of a church building because the audience is usually made up of seekers. However, this method of evangelism may be better served in someone's home, unless the church environment has the comforts of a home atmosphere. It is important that the youth have a safe place to be open and vulnerable with each other and the facilitator. They must be welcomed to come with all of their "baggage," their outrageous hairstyles and clothing, and their pierced and tattooed bodies. But they must also learn to respect the environment, especially in terms of their language and revealing clothing. Within each group, the participants learn to care for, love, and pray for one another, building community from within so that they may build community from without. With this method of evangelism, there has to be an accountability factor, wherein at the end of each session, the participants are asked to make a decision to follow Jesus Christ.

DRAMA EVANGELISM

Our postmodern youth are extremely creative and talented. This method of evangelism utilizes and channels their talents and gifts to proclaim the gospel message in very appealing ways. Those who have artistic abilities can be encouraged to draw or paint their understanding/interpretation of the gospel stories (i.e., the birth of Jesus, the feeding of the five thousand, making fishers of men, the parable of the lost pearl, the baptism of Jesus). Others can create rhythmic lyrics about the gospel message and its interpretation, and apply music to it or create poetry. Still others can be a part of acting out various parables and giving their interpretations, or any other parts of the gospel message.

These are just a few of the many methods of evangelism that we engaged to attract our youth to the Gospel and convince them of its reality. As time goes on, we at TUCC will tap the creative minds of our young people that they may show us how to attract their peers, in Spirit and in truth.

My brother Brian brought his marionette puppets to Trinity as he presented a seminar on Puppetry in the Church. My wife Bridget assisted him on the piano with a dramatic presentation of the song "Smile" by Charlie Chaplin.

Trinity's Grace-Filled Puppets minister in word and song during worship.

A METHODOLOGY OF DISCIPLESHIP IN A POSTMODERN CONTEXT

Discipleship is the weakest component of church growth, yet it is the most critical. (And it will be the most difficult to implement.) It is within discipleship that spiritual growth occurs. The goal of our discipleship is to produce Spirit-filled believers who have entered into God's sovereign rule and reign over their lives.

Discipleship, as previously stated (Chapter 6), is a lifetime process of individual and collective growth in the church. It is within the context of discipleship that believers are sustained and mature toward conforming to the character of Christ. Paul says that if we are to be true followers of Christ, we must have the same attitude as Christ: one of humility, obedience, and servanthood (Phil. 2:5-8). However, in order to have the same attitude as Christ, we must allow ourselves to be discipled by Christ, through the Word of God, under the care of those whom He has called to disciple.

Discipleship begins with a thorough understanding of Jesus' expectations for a disciple. One must begin to adhere to the code of ethics that Jesus set forth in the Beatitudes (Matt. 5:3-11). The introduction to discipleship is understanding and adhering to the *Sermon on the Mount*—Jesus' teachings on discipleship. This is why initiation into the Kingdom of God, as a part of the evangelism process, is so important here. Without being under the sovereign rule and reign of God, understanding and adhering to the teachings in the *Sermon on the Mount* is impossible.

In its postmodern context, discipleship training must be sensitive to the struggles and circumstances in an individual's life, both past and present. Sensitivity is critical, so that this generation, that has problems with absolute truth, trust, and authority, does not backslide, but is encouraged to forge ahead in the name of Jesus Christ. The most effective way to implement discipleship training is through small groups ministry. Because of the enormity of discipleship training and the massive challenges that it presents to this postmodern generation, small groups (4-7 persons) are essential. Group facilitators must definitely themselves be true disciples of Christ and be properly trained to handle the many "twists and turns" that will arise.

In a postmodern context, it is important for the disciples to understand the spiritual gifts bestowed by God the Father, God the Son, and God the Holy Spirit. Every believer has been graced with at least one innate gift from the Father. These gifts are outlined in Romans 12:6-8. Each believer should be "inventoried" and prayerfully lifted up, to learn which of these gifts he may have. As previously mentioned, Jesus has given gifts to the church as *apostles*, *prophets*, *evangelists*, *pastors*, and *teachers*. Every believer needs to have an understanding of the role these gifts play in the life of the church. The Holy Spirit gives nine supernatural manifestations to whom He pleases, as He pleases (1 Cor. 12:7-11). These manifestations are for Spirit-filled believers to be empowered in their living, their evangelism, and their discipleship. Knowing about, understanding, and utilizing these gifts assures every believer that God is indeed alive and well in his life.

TUCC is preparing to engage in three aspects of discipleship training: inductive Bible study, mentoring, and accountability. All three of these aspects will be carried out through small groups ministry.

Our church camp Laurelview, in Somerset county PA provides a welcoming atmosphere and small group evangelism that builds faith and community in our youth ministry. I have participated as a director and counselor at our camp with our youth and churches for over 30 years.

INDUCTIVE BIBLE STUDY

Bible study in-and-of-itself will be a real challenge for this postmodern generation. Since there are several English translations of the Bible, one must be chosen whose "English" is least confusing. The other great challenge is the language of the Bible. That is, the various genres in which the Bible is written. Still another challenge is the irrelevance of the biblical era and culture to the postmodern era and culture. Our facilitators must know and understand the various genres of the Bible and be able to convey this understanding to this generation. Understanding the genre will help many to get past the different styles of writing that they will encounter. Our facilitators must be creative and savvy enough to explain and translate (or analogize) the agricultural references as well as the cultural references throughout the Bible, so that a postmodern, technology-oriented, suburban youth will be able to grasp it and relate to it. The facilitators must be open to the very difficult questions that our young people will ask.

Inductive Bible study is a formational method of Bible study. Under this method, the facilitator guides the participants through a pericope of Scripture through four techniques: *observation*, *interpretation*, *personalization*, and *application*. The participants are no longer inactive zombies who sit and listen and then walk away more perplexed than ever.

During the *observation phase*, the participants engage the text individually as the facilitator asks observation questions for which the answers can be found in the text: who, what, where, how, or why. These observation questions may even involve identifying causes and effects, contrasts, word groupings, etc.

After the observation phase, the facilitator guides the participants into the *interpretation phase* through a series of interpretive questions. Before this phase the facilitator may need to give a mini-presentation on some concept in the text so that an articulate interpretation can be given.

The observation and interpretation phases help the participants to understand the original meaning of the selected passage of Scripture. Once the participants understand the passage itself, the facilitator can move on to the next phases: personalization and application. In both of these phases, the participant not only engages the text but he dialogues with other group members about the text.

The *personalization phase* allows the participant to bring the text into his present day. Here the facilitator asks specific, but general, questions that will help the participants to grope with the text in a more personal way. The participants come face-to-face and are personal with God through His Word and His Spirit dwelling in them.

The *application phase* connects with the personalization phase. The facilitator now challenges each participant to bring alive the responses she/he gave during the personalization phase. The facilitator does this by asking *how* the participant will *apply* what she/he understood and personalized in her/his life in the upcoming week. This phase challenges the participant to truly follow Christ and becomes an accountability factor in her/his life.

Inductive Bible study brings out the meaning of the passage of Scripture chosen. The text is thoroughly analyzed (as much as the participants can tolerate at their level of maturity), leaving little room for reading into the text that which is not really there. It also helps diminish the fears and apprehensions that this postmodern generation may have about God's Word. It would be easier to develop the lessons for this type of study topically. One suggestion is that our youth would better relate to the fact that God has always been interested in young people. The stories of Joseph, David, Esther, Ruth, and Mary center around teenagers and deal with such issues as sibling rivalry, jealousy, loyalty, obedience to God, sex, and bridging the generation gap.

Most importantly, those who are going to facilitate Bible study sessions with this postmodern generation must enculturate postmodernism. They "hang out" with the youth, constantly dialoguing with them about their world and their cultural language. Youthful television programs, such as *13 Reasons Why* and *Gilmore Girls*, give insight into the thinking and mores of this postmodern generation. The facilitator who can engage the youth, learn from them, and bring their world into the Bible study in such a way as to engage in dialogue with God's Word, will be the successful facilitator.

Trust and relationship in Bible study will be the foundation for learning. The believer will be shaped, and thus transformed, by the living Word coming alive in his life. Our Bible Study revolves around three concise and clear steps - (1) OPEN (2) DIG and (3) APPLY. As the facilitator and the participants express and demonstrate a willingness to pray and persist in prayer, they can be confident that God will use His Word to change lives, even in a postmodern world.

MENTORING

Jesus told His disciples, "You call me 'Teacher' and 'Lord' and rightly so, for that is what I am. Now that I, your Lord and Teacher, have washed your feet, you also should wash one another's feet. *I have set you an example that you should do as I have done for you*" (John 13:13-15, emphasis mine). Mentorship involves mature disciples setting an example before infant disciples so that they can mature and also be examples before others. A mentor sows information and a transforming life into the disciple. Postmodern Christians are starving for such attention and human interaction. Living in a fast-paced, get-it-quick society, surrounded by the impersonal nature of technology, leaves one starving for a sense of balance and mental settling.

Many of our youth live in a state of crisis. A true mentor will have compassion for the disciple and try to connect himself with the disciple. He has a craving to share. Mentors question, challenge, listen, and pray for the new believer. This is a sincere and authentic relationship. Mentors reproduce dedication and maturity in a disciple, leaving a legacy that multiplies.

Mentoring is biblical. Moses mentored Joshua, who became the next prophet to succeed Moses as the leader of the Israelites (Joshua 1:1-5). Naomi was a mentor to her daughter-in-law, Ruth, even after her husband had died. She was such a strong mentor that Ruth refused to go back to her people, the Moabites, opting to remain with her mentor (Ruth 1:1-22). Elijah's mentoring of Elisha was so profound that when asked by Elijah (before his translation) what he could do for him, Elisha requested "a double portion of your spirit" (2 Kings 2:1-9). Paul perceived Timothy as a true brother and discipled him into pastoralship. Paul's mentoring was such that he penned Timothy letters of direction and compassion, which today are part of the biblical canon (1 and 2 Timothy). Though these biblical mentors lived in a different time and culture, the principle remains the same. The Apostle Paul wrote, "the things you have heard me say in the presence of many witnesses entrust to reliable men who will also be qualified to teach others" (2 Tim. 2:2).

At TUCC, mentoring is integrated into the small group ministry that incorporates inductive Bible study. In this way, the facilitator of the small group is entrusted to the whole spiritual lives of his constituents. This is what Jesus did. He had a small group—the Twelve—whom He taught and mentored for three years. The facilitator gets involved with the "whole" of the persons in her/his group.

A mentor is not a friend. Friends seek comfort; mentors are corrective. A mentor, by the power of the Holy Spirit (the greatest Mentor in the universe), will incubate and give birth to the disciple's transformation. A true disciple is in pursuit of his mentor's wisdom and faith.

ACCOUNTABILITY

Accountability must be guided by the principles of the Word of God through responsible and trustworthy Christians. In the postmodern world, a student may rebel against unfounded authority. This generation does not respect someone because of their title or position. Authority must be matched with a worthy lifestyle. Trust must overcome suspicion. Postmodern people are serious critical thinkers. They are taught to question everything. Consequently, they have come to believe that there is no absolute truth. Christian accountability is a balance between caring compassion and correct living. Only a total reliance on the Holy Spirit can create such an environment. Postmodern discipleship will not only cherish this relationship, but will enthusiastically lead others to know Christ in this way.

Accountability is not hierarchical. Every disciple (including clergy) is subject to accountability. Therefore, it makes sense that accountability should be maintained more closely at the group level, with the facilitator being held responsible for the accountability of his group members. For several years, I led what I called, the "Para-Clete Mentoring Group" (*paracletus*-Greek word meaning "Helper" for the Holy Spirit's work, in John 14:26; 15:26) in peoples' homes. We were able to mentor new people for leadership and growth in their Christian faith. Within the group, each member held the others, including the facilitator, accountable to Christ-like conduct and the disciple's code of ethics.

CONCLUSION

TUCC has chosen to listen to, include, and empower a generation immersed in a postmodern world. We are at a critical time when we must rethink how we disciple postmodern people. A church built on bureaucracy and stagnated programs is irrelevant. On the other hand, a community of Christians discipling each other in an atmosphere conducive to dialogue and authenticity will share tomorrow's church. Are we ready to take the plunge and offer a forum where the Gospel is taught and people sense God's love?

At TUCC, before we can begin to disciple in a postmodern context, we must truly ask ourselves if we are really prepared for such an endeavor. This is a very serious undertaking because, in a sense, we are "raising" God's children to become mature and responsible spiritual adults. The children follow the adults' examples. Therefore, we must critically ask the hard questions and give honest answers. Have we ourselves become true followers of Christ? Do we understand and adhere to Jesus' code of ethics and teachings for disciples? We cannot afford a "hit-and-miss" discipleship ministry, with the blind leading the blind.

Evangelism and discipleship are not to be a burden for the pastor. Nowhere in the Word of God does Jesus call pastors alone to disciple. In the *Great Commission*, Jesus spoke to eleven *disciples* (not pastors), after He had ordained them *apostles* (not pastors). He knew that they would not live forever, which is why He commanded them to "make disciples." In Ephesians 4:8-12, Paul reminds us that Jesus gave *gifts* to the *church* in the form of *apostles*, *prophets*, *evangelists*, *pastors*, and *teachers*. These *gifts* were given in order that others in the church would be equipped for the service of ministry (evangelism and discipleship). The burden is on *all* whom Jesus has called as gifts, as well as those "saints" who have been equipped (discipled). Evangelism and discipleship are team ministries to bring about church growth in its absolute fullness.

CHAPTER EIGHT

PRACTICAL IMPLEMENTATION OF THE PLAN

A practical implementation of church growth at TUCC dares to face the reality of where we are in regards to reaching this postmodern generation. TUCC has committed its people, time, and resources to embark upon this endeavor. From an evangelist perspective, TUCC has developed an evangelism strategy by providing a more contemporary worship service on Sunday morning. However, our worship services do not exhaust our evangelism intentions. TUCC must utilize other methods of evangelism to reach those who are turned off by the institutional church. We must literally step out of our box and reach out to those who will not voluntarily come to us.

A method for both evangelism and discipleship training that TUCC favors and has already implemented is *small groups ministry*. Small groups facilitate spiritual growth. They are vital in nourishing the ministry of the laity in the congregation. James admonishes us: "Do not merely listen to the word, and so deceive yourselves. Do what it says" (Jas. 1:22). Small groups encourage every believer to become a disciple by following Christ in doing what His Word says. The remainder of this chapter will first give a historical background of small groups ministry at TUCC. I then discuss the assimilation and cultivation of new members. Finally, I enter into a serious discussion of what needs to be enhanced, deleted, and added in order that TUCC can have more effective small groups. Groups that will fully utilize our strategic evangelism and discipleship methodologies, while implementing our core values in an effort to "win, disciple, and serve."

A HISTORY OF SMALL GROUPS MINISTRY AT TUCC

TUCC has always had small groups. There were men and women groups and Sunday school classes. Children and youth naturally gathered into groups that focused on their needs. Even an MS (multiple sclerosis) support group met at the church. These groups placed their primary emphasis on relational and emotional well-being.

As part of our leadership training, we invited Dr. David Roadcup to share his insight and wisdom on how to organize a small groups ministry. His church in Atlanta grew with an emphasis on small groups ministry. We knew that we needed to train quality leaders to lead the groups. Therefore, we gathered a talented cluster of TUCC members to structure this kind of ministry. A detailed plan was created to train facilitators to lead groups of eight to twelve people. The emphasis would include fellowship, Bible study, and prayer. The groups would meet weekly during the school year and be off during the summer.

The purpose of our small groups ministry was threefold. First, it provided a teaching environment, using the *Serendipity* series by Lyman Coleman.[127] Second, it instituted prayer as a lifeline for support. As Icenogle states, "Prayer is the primary discipline of the Christian group. Without prayer there is little hope that the group will come to grips with its primary purposes for gathering."[128] Third, intentional discipleship takes place, which leads to transformation. The groups are serious about their faith and are not afraid to make a commitment to relational accountability. It was our hope that small groups in our church would discover their potential to grow and serve Jesus Christ. In this way, they would contribute to the spiritual growth of the entire congregation.

THE IMPLEMENTATION OF SMALL GROUPS AT TUCC

> It was he [Jesus Christ] who gave some to be apostles, some to be prophets, some to be evangelists, and some to be pastors and teachers, *to prepare God's people for works of service*, so that the body of Christ might be built up until we all reach unity in the faith and in the knowledge of the Son of God and become mature, attaining the full measure of perfection found in Christ. (Eph. 4:11-13, emphasis mine)

God's intention is for His appointed ministers to facilitate lay initiatives that will empower the members of the Body of Christ. This is to equip all of God's people to do ministry, works of service. However, the institutional churches have

127 Lyman Coleman, *The Serendipity Series* (Nashville: Serendipity House), http://www.serendipity.com. The Serendipity curriculum focuses on relational small groups dynamics combined with intentional Bible study. The organization wants to give Christians material to help them grow while on their spiritual journey. There are literally hundreds of different books, booklets, and pamphlets for Bible study leaders to pick from. Each facilitator/disciple covenants with the people in the small groups about what material to buy and share with the group.

128 Gareth V. Icenogle, *Biblical Foundations for Small Groups Ministry* (Downers Grove: InterVarsity, 1994), 137.

misinterpreted the above Scripture and deceived the people of God. The purpose of the *fivefold ministry* is *not* to do ministry, as works of service. The purpose of the *fivefold ministry* (not just pastors!) is to *prepare God's people* so that *they* may do the works of service.

At TUCC, the goal is to give permission for the laity to do ministry by being obedient to Christ's mandate in Ephesians 4:11, 12. In most churches, the pastor does most of the ministry, while the majority of the congregation either sits back and watch or complain, or dictates to the "leadership."

> The greatest need in evangelical churches is the release of members for ministry. A Gallup survey discovered that only 10 percent of American church members are active in any kind of personal ministry and that 50 percent of all church members have no interest in serving in any ministry. . . . The encouraging news that Gallup uncovered this: 40 percent of all members have expressed an interest in having a ministry, but they have never been asked or they don't know how. This group is an untapped gold mine! If we can mobilize this 40 percent and add them to the current 10 percent already serving, your church could have 50 percent of its members active in ministry.[129]

TUCC believes in the concept of every member in ministry. We preach about it and even help our members discover their spiritual gifts. The church must be moved by the immense physical and spiritual needs of people and the call of Christ to minister. Mobilizing the laity for ministry ensures growth for the ministry.

---

129 Rick Warren, *The Purpose Driven Church* (Grand Rapids: Zondervan, 1995), 365-66.

The clergy are part of the problem. We have codependent habits which subconsciously tells us to take on the church's and other peoples' problems, rather than delegate that "authority" to qualified others who are not clergy. In the Old Testament, Moses was codependent, until his father-in-law, Jethro, enlightened him. Moses held expectations that were beyond his abilities. Moses said, "The people come to me to seek God's will. Whenever I decide they have a dispute, it is brought to me, and I decide between the parties and inform them of God's decrees and laws" (Exod. 18:15, 16). However, Jethro retorted, "What you are doing is not good. You and these people who come out to you will only wear yourselves out. The work is too heavy for you; you cannot handle it alone" (Exod. 18:17, 18). Moses replied that he was only doing what was asked of him, however, he allowed the people to define his leadership role.

Just as Moses, subconsciously and out of inexperience, implied to the Hebrews that he had to handle every problem and situation in his leadership role, so has the pastor with regard to the parishioners. Although Jesus implemented team ministry for the Church (Eph. 4:11, 12), pastors have dominated that leadership, pushing out the other four members of the "team." Not only that, we have set up an emotional contract with the laity that cannot be fully honored. A pastor who accepts the codependent model will rarely produce a growing church. An emotional dependency is created that will keep the people as spiritual children and never allow them to grow in the faith.

As the senior pastor, I must create healthy boundaries to release the people for ministry. Keith Miller clearly states, "Boundaries keep people from abusing us, bursting into our space and controlling us or getting us to do things before we have a chance to think or say no. Our boundaries also keep us aware of others' boundaries so that we do not break into their God-given space to control or abuse them."[130] I learned to delegate responsibility and share ministry with the laity. Only a concerted and intentional effort can create a new model that is both biblical and healthy. Lay ministry at TUCC will best be promoted and encouraged by the pastor through his sermons and Bible study.

ASSIMILATION OF MEMBERS

New members are not immediately assigned to a small group. That would be spiritual genocide, especially for this postmodern generation of youth and young adults. Their initial orientation into the life of the church is called assimilation, and is done through an assimilation course called *Trinity 101.*

Assimilation is the process of moving people from an awareness of TUCC to responsible church attendance and active membership. At TUCC, we are aiming to give the members a sense of ownership, as they contribute their lives to the cause of Christ. Lyle Schaller writes,

> There is considerable evidence that suggests that at least one-third, and perhaps as many as one-half, of all Protestant church members do not feel a sense of belonging to the congregation of which they are members. They have been received into membership. but have never felt they have been accepted into the fellowship circle.[131]

At TUCC, we want all of our new members to be in fellowship with each other and the whole of our church. To support this effort, we have devised a class called *Trinity 101.* A weak membership class will build a weak congregation. A strong class

130 Keith Miller, *A Hunger for Healing.* San Francisco: Harper Collins, 1992), 235.

131 Lyle Schaller, *Assimilating New Members* (Nashville: Abingdon, 1983), 16.

will be a great starting point to build a healthy congregation of disciples. *Trinity 101* answers several questions: (1) What are the benefits and responsibilities of being a member at TUCC? (2) What is the mission of TUCC, specifically? and (3) How is the church organized and how can I be a part of her ministry? This class is held four times a year.

The class is divided into four sessions. The first session presents a general introduction to the Christian Church (Disciples of Christ) denomination. We want to be up-front about the affiliation and accountability of the church.

The second session shares specifically what TUCC is about, who we are. We communicate the doctrinal beliefs of TUCC and that our leaning is evangelical, though we are a mainline church. We desire people to understand the value and meaning of membership. It is not just shaking the minister's hand at the closing of a worship service and having one's name on a church's membership roll. If we can share with them the enthusiasm Christ has given us, we believe that we can open their hearts to be a part of our church experience. Our fellowship with them will meet an inner need to belong to something greater than themselves.

The third session involves the practical application of their lives to TUCC. We give an overview of the Trinitarian gifts as presented in C. Peter Wagner's book, *Your Spiritual Gifts Can Help Your Church Grow.*[132] A simple gifts survey is given to each participant. After they take the survey they are given an overview of their orientation as a Christian. Gifts such as administration, mercy, giving and prophecy are "inventoried." We want each person to find his place and utilize his gifts at TUCC. We will not fill slots or openings just because they are there. In our view,

132 C. Peter Wagner, *Your Spiritual Gifts Can Help Your Church Grow* (Ventura, CA: Regal Books, 1994).

this is akin to heresy. When a church places people in situations where they are gifted, the church is misusing the privileges God has given to share His ministry to the world.

The fourth session is actual assimilation. The question that they must address is, "Where you do fit into TUCC?" After his understanding of the denomination, our church doctrine, and his gifts, the new member is gently, but strongly, encouraged to assimilate into the ministry of the church where his gifts will be best utilized. God does not want us to grow in isolation from each other.

The next act of assimilation is still in the development stage. We are creating a *membership covenant* which will share the commitment one is making to TUCC and the Church universal. The membership covenant will be similar to a marriage vow. In marriage, a man and woman exchange vows and promises are made before God and His people. This covenant is the true essence of the marriage. In like manner, the essence of church membership is a spiritual covenant where one commits w before God, to the church. The membership class will focus on commitment and provide the necessary accountability. Jan Linn, pastor of the Spirit of Joy Christian Church in Minneapolis, Minnesota, writes, "The strength of covenant membership is that it yokes people together to share the burden of the journey, and that gives us strength we do not otherwise have."[133] As each person individually prays and seeks God's guidance about how she/he can be a part of TUCC, we as a church pray that God will direct the people He wants us to meet and connect with His purposes.

133 Jan Linn, *Rocking the Church Membership Boat: Counting Members or Having Members Who Count* (St. Louis: Chalice Press, 2001), 74.

THE CULTIVATION OF NEW MEMBERS

The new members classes involve our visitors and guests. Although, over the period of the two classes, friendships are formed between some of the new members, they must still assimilate into the church (fellowshipping with other members) in order to be "cultivated" (discipled). TUCC wants to prevent isolation of new members from the mainstream of the church. Therefore, TUCC has a commitment to assign and involve each new member in a small group.

New members do not become assimilated to the congregation until they feel a sense of belonging. Our small groups ministry is called *Life Groups* and is the key to expressing quality care in the church. Our small groups ministry provides care that cannot be provided on Sunday morning. These small groups break down the remainder of the assimilation process into manageable sizes so that people can better care for each other.

With this intentional procedure for assimilation, we have closed the back door of the church. We now have over twenty groups which people can join and feel the care of Christ and His people. We will have less worries as we connect people with a group. Every member will share in the work of the ministry and grow in the spiritual gifts God has given.

CONCLUSION

After having researched the biblical foundations for church growth and developing a theology for the same, I collaborated with some of my colleagues and came up with some methodologies for evangelism and discipleship. Although TUCC is growing, both spiritually and numerically, there is lots of room for improving on what we now have. Although TUCC has given much thought to attending to the spiritual needs of the postmodern sect of our congregation, what we are doing may not be enough to sustain them. From what I have learned from my research and subsequent conversations, I believe that TUCC should rethink its small groups ministry, to be more effective in the postmodern world. Small groups are definitely the way to do lay ministry in order to achieve the fullness of evangelism and discipleship. Perhaps TUCC needs to restructure its small groups ministry so that it becomes the dominant source for doing evangelism and discipleship. In other words, each member of TUCC becomes a member of only one small group, wherein they are ministered to and prepared to do ministry. The initial assimilation into small groups might include further evangelistic endeavors, mainly initiation into the Kingdom of God. This could include Bible studies on what the Kingdom of God, in this life, entails and the implications of it for the disciples. Because the Gospel of Jesus Christ is the Kingdom of God, it is critical to one's understanding of God's plan of salvation and one's relationship with God.

Questions that postmodern youth and young adults are likely to ask may be: Why did God choose to become a human being in Jesus Christ? How did Jesus' death on the cross, over two thousand years ago, atone for my sins today? How do I communicate with God and build this relationship with Him? If God is so good and loves us so much, why is the world so crazy and evil? Why do bad things happen to good people? There may be many, many more as they struggle to come to grips with their new creation in Christ Jesus, in a world that has run amuck.

New members can also learn in their small groups how to engage in personal evangelism without intimidating their friends and families with their zealousness. They are encouraged to exercise their gifts in an effort to be creative witnesses in the world. Other guided evangelistic endeavors can be engaged on a group basis. Each small group can commit to a project of silent evangelism and prayer evangelism coupled with individual, personal evangelism.

Chapter 7 gave an elaborate discussion of discipleship methodology. Discipleship is implemented through small groups. The facilitator and the small group are the same as the one in evangelism. The members bond with each other and the facilitator, loving and caring for each other in spiritual fellowship and worship. The facilitator is not only the "extended evangelist" for each member of his group, but also each member's teacher and mentor.

God has great expectations for His church. He expects every Christian to use his talents for His glory. Our greatest need and objective are to release the congregation to do the work of the ministry. As people become interested and involved, their investment will be the glue that holds to each other and to our Lord. Assimilation can happen when authentic Christians reach out to new people with unconditional love and intentional faith.

No methodology or ministry is fool-proof, because we are all imperfect beings. However, certain measures must be put into place to ensure that small groups do not become isolated "cliques" in the church, stagnating true assimilation into the whole life of the church. One way to ensure that this does not happen might be to have a whole congregational social gathering on a quarterly basis so that all members can mingle with and get to know each other a little better. Also, the small groups would not include Sunday school. Sunday school will be deliberately set up so that each class will not constitute an original small group, but will have participants who are from various small groups as well as those visiting our church.

Another measure to keep small groups from being self-contained is implementing a method of multiplication. The result of making disciples is for the disciples to "go and make disciples." One of the responsibilities of the facilitator is to groom and identify the readiness of each group member to become a facilitator. Each group member is expected to become a facilitator of a newly formed small group (in approximately 6-12 months). This makes clear sense, as we project monumental growth at TUCC. In addition, the new facilitator remains a member of his original small group and continues to attend those sessions in order to maintain accountability and to receive the support and encouragement of those who know him so well. Disciples making disciples. This is our ultimate goal at TUCC.

CONCLUSION

> No one pours new wine into old wineskins. If he does, the new wine will burst the skins, the wine will run out and the wineskins will be ruined. No, new wine must be poured into new wineskins. And no one, after drinking the old wine wants the new, for he says, 'The old is better.' (Luke 5:37-39)

Can TUCC be a model for traditional churches in western Pennsylvania? Will the postmodern generation be left behind as the church stands still? Can we outline a new pattern of thinking that can adapt to the postmodern context? Can conflicting ideas such as rational/relational and physical/spiritual exist simultaneously? These are the questions people must answer today or our communities will have numerous churches as historical markers in the future.

Tradition and history are wonderful subjects. We love to remember and pass on our stories. As the old axiom states, "Those who do not learn from history are doomed to repeat it." Inherent within that statement is the idea that the principles of history are important, not the outward trappings. Today, we are in a new era of history. In essence, I am stating the same concept in a peculiar context, the church. Growing a church in a staunch traditional region of the country is an incredible challenge. In Matthew 28:18-20, our Lord commands us to go into all the world; however, he does not give us a formula to follow. Rather, he charges us to take His saving and healing message to lost people. Again, his Word never changes, but the method of presentation may vary from person to person, and from era to era, culture to culture. If we do not adapt our methods we stand the risk of becoming museums and nostalgic memories from the past.

In the 1980s, a prophecy was given concerning the city of Pittsburgh and the surrounding communities. It stated that "someday Pittsburgh will be known as much for God as it is for steel." Yes, the economy and steel industry have declined in the area, but peoples' need for God has never waned. We have an incredible message that has been entrusted to us. At the heart of it is Jesus: His life, teaching, death and resurrection. TUCC has been on a journey to discover new ways to reach the postmodern world. The Holy Spirit is opening the hearts of His people to do a new work in New Kensington and Lower Burrell. This book has been an investigation into this process.

TUCC is a complex organism. It was a merger of two different congregations, mixed with evangelical and charismatic influences. Thus, can a church with such diversity continue to forge ahead? We believe that strong pastoral and lay leadership is the glue to hold it together. Without training in both evangelism and discipleship, our vision and mission will subside. In addition, a risk-taking faith with Christ's power is required to move this traditional church to the cutting edge of church growth.

Change has been one of the biggest forces to overcome at TUCC. The western Pennsylvania culture changes very little;

the church follows even slower. Hence, much effort and energy has been given to this body of believers, called TUCC, to help it grow. We have taken momentous steps of courage and God has blessed each act of faith. As a mainline church, we have much to offer other churches in the area regarding evangelism. We are continuing to grow spiritually in discipleship of the entire congregation. Yet, until we combine both forces with a passion for the Kingdom of God, we will never become the church God created us to be.

As was stated in this book, our goal is not merely numbers. We will lose the integrity of our vision if counting people is the end result. Evangelism without biblical discipleship is fruitless. Our present objective is to build strong spiritual development in the lives of the people. Through this process, we will see not only the life of the congregation blossom, but God Himself will bring more people to share in His *Great Commission*.

As we learn how to incarnate the "good news" of the Gospel to our community, Jesus will make disciples who will communicate His love with others. Our Lord's call to "Follow Me" will eventually lead us to the cross and the resurrection. True and authentic discipleship will bear both fruit and consecrated sacrifice. As a result, we will glorify God and live out the purpose God created for our lives.

Because TUCC's history is rich with tradition, we have many senior citizens in our membership. We never wanted to push them out of the church. That action would be diametrically opposed to God's admonition to honor your elders (1 Tim. 5:17). However, we recognize that a new generation of people are in our congregation. Many young people have come from divorced families. Many of them do not know what it means to have a mom, dad, or grandparents. They are seeking spirituality, yet they do not recognize or relate to the American church culture of the early twentieth century. Our goal to reach postmodern folks comes, not from a rebellious heart, but rather a compassion to reach lost souls for God's Kingdom. We need to wake up to this new world and establish a rapport with a rapidly changing globe. The twenty-first century is here. There is a plethora of ideas swirling in our communities. People cannot cope with the changes. That is why we have invested so much time and energy into new music, youth ministry, and leadership skills. A multigenerational church can provide the spiritual family needed for a new generation of people. Through evangelism and discipleship, we are continuing to empower the laity (both youth and adults) to be ministers in their world. The human need that hungers and thirsts for God is never quenched. If we can lay aside our pride and peer into a human soul, the call to share the Gospel will be simple: go and make disciples (Matt. 28:18-20). We proclaim Christ and He convicts hearts by the Holy Spirit. Our responsibility is to obey; His initiative is to transform. In short, we at TUCC are missionaries to a field that is ready to be harvested.

Our slogan, *Winning, Discipling, Serving* sums up TUCC's mission. It is our vision, mission, and strategy tied up in one phrase. It is not motivational fluff. Every ministry at TUCC must commit their work to prayer. Then, with others of similar spiritual gifts, create a tangible strategy. Ultimately, the motives and beliefs must fall under the umbrella of our motto. Likewise, both the elders and board must be shaped by this attitude. Finally, myself as the pastor must intentionally and directly proclaim to the flock that winning souls, discipling Christians, and serving people is our aim. I will be accountable to this eternal goal. The core values that TUCC leaders chose, undergird our slogan. *Worship* leads us into the presence of God. *Spiritual development* will disciple each person individually to grow into a mature, committed Christian. *Stewardship* tells us that everything we have belongs to God. Therefore, we must commit ourselves—body, mind, and spirit—to Christ's purpose for our lives. So that finally, our lives are lived in *mission* and sacrifice. Following this path, we truly will journey with Jesus, all the way to the cross.

TUCC has the potential for a fantastic future. In the past, every time the congregation dared to trust God, He showed up in supernatural ways. We want to allow God to surprise us again! Are we ready to embrace the postmodernists in our neighborhoods? Can intentional multicultural and family ministries happen? Revelation 21:26 says, "the glory and honor of the nations will be brought into it." This chapter is a description of heaven. One day the differences that divide us will be affirmed by the Creator of the universe. We can begin this process in this lifetime.

My role as a pastor must begin with a prayerful and humble heart, seeking God's guidance to direct this church. Certainly, the people of Trinity are the real ministers who will reach their spheres of influence for our Lord! I have shared with the congregation on many Sundays, these three exhortations,

"I have three goals as a pastor for each one of you,

(1) Learn to hear God's voice (read and study the Bible-that is God speaking to you)

(2) Discover your spiritual gift

(3) Now, go and live out God's will in your life!"

I believe TUCC can become a model church to our community and denomination. We are taking the best of both worlds: the traditional and postmodern. We are challenging the people to think outside the box. Our supreme goal is to save souls for

Jesus. Our privilege is to enter into the greatest mission on earth. We are on an exciting process to discover the unique way God is releasing and expanding His kingdom through TUCC. We are His instruments. May God use us to fulfill His intentions and end in our lives as we, "Go and make disciples of all nations, baptizing them in the name of the Father and of the Son and of the Holy Spirit, and teaching them to obey everything I have commanded you" (Matt. 28:19-20). This command of our Lord reveals THE CALL of evangelism and discipleship that we are endeavoring to implement at Trinity, for the glory of God!

Getting ready to give a message for worship. Our message of Christ's love on the cross never changes, but our methods must touch people's lives in the present moment! Let's go REACH, TOUCH, and BLESS our generation for Jesus Christ!

BIBLIOGRAPHY

Abraham, William J. *The Logic of Evangelism*. Grand Rapids: Eerdmans, 1989.

Anderson, Leith. *A Church for the 21st Century*. Minneapolis: Bethany House, 1992.

Ardnt, William F. and F. Wilbur Gingrich. *A Greek-English Lexicon of the New Testament and Other Early Christian Literature*, 2d ed. Chicago: University of Chicago Press, 1979.

Barna, George. *Church Marketing: Breaking Ground for the Harvest*. Ventura, CA: Regal Books, 1992.

________. *The Power of Vision*. Ventura, CA: Regal Books, 1992.

Barrett, David B. "Evangelize! An Historical Survey of the Concept." *Global Evangelization Movement: The AD 2000 Series*. Birmingham: New Hope, 1987.

Bateman, Rose and Irene Love. *Trinity United Church History*. August 1995.

Becker, U. "Gospel, Evangelize, Evangelist." Pages 107-112 in vol. 2 of *The New International Dictionary of New Testament Theology*. Edited by Colin Brown. 4 vols. Grand Rapids: Zondervan, 1975-1985.

Bronner, Edwin B. *William Penn's "Holy Experiment."* New York: Temple University Publications, 1962.

Callahan, Kennon. *Dynamic Worship*. San Francisco: Jossey-Bass, 1997.

________. *Twelve Keys to an Effective Church*. San Francisco: Harper&Row, 1983.

Coleman, Lyman. *The Serendipity Series*. Nashville: Serendipity House. http://www.serendipity.com.

Coleman, Robert E. "Theology of Evangelism." *Review & Expositor* 77 (Fall 1980): 473-481.

Constitution of Trinity United Christian Church. New Kensington, PA: 1998.

Craig, Robert H. and Robert C. Worley. *Dry Bones Live: Helping Congregations Discover New Life*. Louisville: John Knox, 1992.

de Jong, Pieter. *Evangelism and Contemporary Theology*. Nashville: Tidings, 1962.

Edgemon, Roy G. "Evangelism and Discipleship." *Review & Expositor* 77 (Fall 1980): 539-547.

Garland, David E. "Evangelism in the New Testament." *Review & Expositor* 77 (Fall 1980): 461-471.

Getz, Gene A. *Sharpening the Focus of the Church*. Chicago: Moody, 1974.

Green, Michael. *Evangelism in the Early Church*. The Mount, Guildford: Inter Publishing Service Ltd, St. Nicholas House, 1995.

Hayford, Jack. *Worship His Majesty: How Praising the King of Kings Will Change Your Life*. Waco, TX: Word Books, 1987; Ventura, CA: Regal Books, 2000.

Hestenes, Roberta. *Turning Committees Into Communities*. Colorado Springs: Navpress, 1993.

Hoekendijk, Johannes C. *The Church Inside Out*. Edited by L. A. Hoedemaker and Pieter Tijmes. Translated by Isaac C. Rottenberg. Philadelphia: Westminister, 1966.

Hunter, George C., III and Bruce Larson. *Church for the Unchurched*. Nashville: Abingdon, 1996.

Icenogle, Gareth W. *Biblical Foundations for Small Group Ministry*. Downers Grove: InterVarsity, 1994.

"It All Started in 1681 with Penn." *The Tribune Review*. No pages. Cited 12 August 2002. Online: http://www.pittsburghlive.com/x/tribune-review/specialreports/regionalism/startedwithpenn.html.

Kelly, Dean M. *Why Conservative Churches are Growing*. San Francisco: Harper&Row, 1972.

Klein, Philip. *A History of Pennsylvania*. Pennsylvania State University. [see footnote]

Lim, D. S. "Evangelism in the Early Church." Pages 353-358 in *Dictionary of the Later New Testament & Its Development*. Edited by Ralph P. Martin and Peter H. Davids. Downers Grove: InterVarsity, 1997.

Linn, Jan. *Rocking the Church Membership Boat: Counting Members or Having Members Who Count*. St. Louis: Chalice, 2001.

Logan, Robert. *Beyond Church Growth*. Old Tappan, NJ: Revell, 1989.

MacNaughton, John H. *Stewardship: Myths and Methods—A Program Guide for Ministers and Lay Leaders*. New York: Seabury, 1975.

Maxwell, John C. *The 21 Irrefutable Laws of Leadership*. Nashville: Thomas Nelson, 1998.

McGavran, Donald and Win Arn. *How to Grow a Church*. Glendale, CA: G/L Publications, 1973.

McLaughlin, Corrine and Gordon Davidson. "The Esoteric Side of the Founding of America."*In Context* 3 (Summer 1983): 7. Cited 12 August 2002. Online: http://www.context.org/ICLIB/IC03/CoriGord.htm.

Meade, Loren. *The Once and Future Church: Reinventing the Congregation for a New Mission Frontier*. New York: The Alban Institute, 1991.

Merriam Webster Online Dictionary. Springfield, MA: Merriam Webster, Inc. http://www.m-w.com/cgi-bin-dictionary.

Meyerbuber, Carl I. *Less Than Forever: The Rise and Decline of Union Solidarity in Western Pennsylvania*. Selinsgrove, PA: Susquehanna University Press, 1987.

Miller, Keith. *A Hunger for Healing*. San Francisco: Harper Collins, 1992.

Morgenthaler, Sally. *Worship Evangelism: Inviting Unbelievers into the Presence of God*. Grand Rapids: Zondervan, 1999.

Muller, D. "*mathetes*—learner, pupil, disciple." Pages 484-490 in vol. 1 of *The New International Dictionary of New Testament Theology*. Edited by Colin Brown. 4 vols. Grand Rapids: Zondervan, 1975-1985.

New International Version [Holy Bible]. Grand Rapids: Zondervan, 1991.

Packer, J. I. *Evangelism and the Sovereignty of God.* Downers Grove: InterVarsity, 1961.

Posterski, Donald. *Reinventing Evangelism: New Strategies for Presenting Christ in Today's World.* Downers Grove: InterVarsity, 1989.

Rainer, Thom S. *The Book of Church Growth: History, Theology and Principles.* Nashville: Broadman Press, 1993.

Ramm, Bernard. "The Theology of Evangelism." In *Occasional Papers,* ed. Darrel L. Guder and James R. Oraker, 150-163. Colorado Springs: Institute of Youth Ministries, 1978.

Richards, Lawrence O. *A Theology of Christian Education.* Grand Rapids: Zondervan, 1975.

Richardson, Rick. *Evangelism Outside the Box: New Ways to Help People Experience the Good News.* Downers Grove: InterVarsity, 2000.

Schaller, Lyle. *Assimilating New Members.* Nashville: Abingdon, 1983.

________. *Parish Planning: How to Get Things Done in the Church.* Nashville: Abingdon, 1971.

Senn, Frank. *The Witness of the Worshipping Community.* New York: Paulist, 1993.

Stott. John R. *Christian Mission in the Modern World.* Downers Grove: InterVarsity, 1976.

Sweazy, George E. *Effective Evangelism.* New York: Harper & Row, 1953.

Sweet, Leonard. "Target the Trends." *Leadership* 14 (Spring 1993): 21-22.

Wagner, C. Peter. *Your Church Can Grow.* Ventura, CA: Regal Books, 1984.

________. *Your Spiritual Gifts Can Help Your Church to Grow.* Ventura, CA: Regal Books, 1994.

Warren, Rick. *The Purpose Driven Church.* Grand Rapids: Zondervan, 1995.

Wilkins, Michael J. "Disciple." Pages 176-182 in *Dictionary of Jesus and the Gospels.* Edited by Joel B. Green and Scot McKnight. Downers Grove: InterVarsity, 1992.

________. "Discipleship." Pages 183-188 in *Dictionary of Jesus and the Gospels.* Edited by Joel B. Green and Scot McKnight. Downers Grove: InterVarsity, 1992.

The Women's Club of New Kensington. *Lore of Yore: A History of New Kensington, Arnold and Lower Burrell.* New Kensington, PA: Buhl Brothers Printing, 1986.

WA